New Nations and Peoples

Turkey

Turkey

ANDREW MANGO

with 35 illustrations and 4 maps

WALKER AND COMPANY
NEW YORK

Library of Congress Catalog Card Number: 68-13999

First published in the United States of America in 1968 by Walker and Company, a division of the Walker Publishing Company, Inc.

Printed in Great Britain by Jarrold and Sons Ltd, Norwich

Contents

Introduction

THERE HAVE BEEN many books written on Turkey. At first the Turkish threat to Christendom compelled attention. Books on the laws and customs of the Turks and on the origin of their empire attempted to explain Turkish victories. Every explanation was also a warning to Christians to close their ranks, to improve their organization, to practise the virtues of their religion. Then, as the Turkish tide was first stemmed, and then pushed back, it was the decline of a once powerful empire which fascinated Western observers. 'The history of the progress and decadence of empires contains many useful lessons, while presenting at the same time a panorama that is both impressive and curious', as a typical nineteenth-century French writer put it.[1] So again there were explanations made and morals drawn. Then came the reforms, urged by European powers and applied by Ottoman governments to arrest the decay of the Empire.

The Ottoman Empire became officially part of the concert of civilized states while remaining the 'sick man' of Europe. Diagnoses, advice for a cure, prognoses of a recovery or, more commonly, of the Empire's demise, poured from the printing presses. And so on to the First World War, the Turkish War of Independence and the foundation of the Turkish Republic, after which Turkey old and new was the subject and, usually, the title of another generation of books.

Yet even when the authors urged the westernization of Turkey or discussed the extent to which that process had already come to pass, it was the differences rather than the similarities between Turkey and Europe which attracted attention. These differences were important in themselves as well as in their consequences, for the importance of Turkey lay in the fact that it was the first non-Christian, non-European

7

society on the confines of Europe. It was pre-eminently a stranger outside the gates, intercourse with whom, in war as well as in peace, helped Europe to define itself and to mould its own personality. Books on Turkey were in this sense also books about Europe. Writers who extolled Turkish virtues decried either explicitly or implicitly the vices of Europe. These were usually the pessimists, the conservatives. Those on the other hand who criticized Turkey usually believed in European progress. They were the liberals, the optimists, the progressives. Most books on Turkey seemed to fall into these two classes – the class of conservative admirers and that of progressive critics. The difference between the two outlooks became more or less institutionalized in the age of Gladstone, when Liberals with a capital L, by espousing the cause of the Christian subjects of the Ottoman Empire, seemed to write off all Turks as unredeemable enemies of progress. Progressive arguments came to cloak racial hostility. However, with the founding of the Republic, the cause of progress became official Turkish policy and attitudes had to be readjusted. Now it was not the Turks as such, but conservative elements among them that attracted criticism, for before long it was seen that the otherness of Turkey had persisted in spite of the change in official policy. The fascination of Turkey was, of course, precisely in that otherness, and certainly travel books relied on it much more than on the country's new Western institutions. Today Turkey differs from countries lying to the west of it in so far as much of Turkish society is still pre-technological. This is not a Turkish characteristic since other developing countries are similarly placed. But there are unique differences too that only the country's history can explain. Even new nations and peoples cannot be properly understood outside their historical context.

In any case is Turkey, or rather are the Turks, a new nation and a new people? Those who would answer in the affirmative would point to the fact that the modern Turkish Republic was founded in 1923. But that Republic was not created from nothing. It was fashioned from the remnants of the Ottoman Empire, which had prevailed in that land for over six centuries and which was commonly and rightly known as Turkey, just as its rulers and the mass of its subjects were usually referred to as Turks. What is more, Turks had ruled much of the territory of the present-day Turkish Republic for two centuries before the foundation of the Ottoman state. If the history of the Turkish Republic started in 1923, its pre-history goes back to 1071 – which is near enough to 1066 to make the Turks about as new a nation as the English. Yet in spite of all those centuries of recognizable historical existence, the Turks today are a new nation in the sense that the English are not.

Newness is of course a matter of definition. Is a stone we pick up in a field old or new? Similarly, when does an existing community become a new nation? Perhaps youthful is a more useful word, for the Turks today are a youthful people, in the literal sense that the young are more numerous among them than they are in England. That, of course, means simply that they have just had the population explosion which Western Europe underwent a century ago. However, Turkey is truly new in many other ways. Most of its political and many of its social institutions are new; its alphabet and even much of its language are new; its official culture is fairly new; all its industry, most of its communications, many of its skills are new. But we can go further and say that in a sense the Turkish nation itself is new. Until recently, more or less until the foundation of the Republic, there were officially no Turks, only Muslims, just as the Ottoman Empire was officially not a Turkish but a Muslim state. It was a state founded specifically to extend the boundaries of Islam and to promote its interests. It was ruled by Muslims, but it was never homogeneously Muslim or Turkish. Like all empires the world has known it was a multi-national, a plural state. The proportion of Turks among its inhabitants is difficult to establish, but it would seem that throughout most of its history, people whom we could fairly call Turks were a minority, although the dominant minority of its inhabitants. As late as 1880, when the Ottoman Empire had lost most of its possessions and, therefore, most of its non-Turkish subjects in Europe, it was estimated that of its 25 million inhabitants only some ten million were Turks, although almost seventeen million were Muslims.[2] True, in the lands which today form the Turkish Republic, the Turks were definitely in the majority, but even in these lands there lived considerable numbers of non-Turks, mainly Greeks and Armenians, whose importance was often out of proportion to their numbers. It was often claimed, for example, that throughout the length and breadth of Turkey, there was not a single Turkish-owned grocer's shop. The Turks were mainly administrators, soldiers and peasants. Today on the other hand the Turks represent over 90 per cent of the population of the Republic and perform all or almost all the functions of a modern society.

The change from a Muslim Turkish community geographically scattered and socially incomplete to a nation that is integrated territorially and has achieved a large measure of social integration is a qualitative change and to this extent the modern Turkish nation is a new organism.

1   Historical Turkey

THE TERRITORY of the modern Turkish Republic was won by
the Turks for Islam in roughly four centuries – between 1071, when
Asia Minor was first successfully invaded by the Turks and large-scale
Turkish settlement began, and 1453 when Constantinople fell to them.
Many more lands lying further to the west were won and then lost, but
the territory of the present-day republic remained the core of the
Turkish state, at whose boundaries the Ottoman retreat stopped and
whose Turkish character has been preserved and developed over at
least five centuries.

This Turkish heartland is more or less coterminous with Asia
Minor – a rectangular peninsula bounded on the north by the Black
Sea, on the west by the Aegean and on the south by the Mediterranean.
The land frontiers in the east and south-east are more difficult to define,
although one can say that in the south-east Turkey starts where the
mountains start and the Mesopotamian plain ends, while in the eastern
marches, the Caspian watershed more or less divides Turkey from
Persia. Asia Minor so defined is a bridge between Asia and Europe,
parts of it being more accessible from the west than from the east. Also,
although a geographical unit, it overlaps with other geographical units
that were once also political units. Thus the basin of the Aegean Sea is
a geographical unit embracing continental and insular Greece as well
as the western coast of Turkey. This is the cradle of the Hellenic world
and of Greek civilization, whose ambiguous eastern frontier was
disputed between Greeks and Persians in antiquity and Greeks and
Turks in modern times. In the north-east, it is equally hard to say where
Asia Minor ends and the Caucasus, or rather Transcaucasia, begins.

Here the frontier between Turks, Georgians, Armenians, Persians and Russians has also been a matter of dispute.

Thus broadly defined, Asia Minor or Anatolia (the East as the Greeks called it) resisted the first great wave of Islamic expansion in the seventh century. Arabs raided deeply into it, as far as Constantinople itself, but they did not establish themselves north of the Taurus range, which forms the southern rampart of Asia Minor. Further east, the uplands of eastern Turkey, or Armenia as it then was, also eluded their grasp. Politically Asia Minor remained part of the Eastern Roman or Byzantine Empire. To the Muslims it was the Land of Rum or Rome. Culturally, it remained Byzantine Greek, a culture difficult to define but drawing certainly on the Christian, as well as on the Hellenic heritage, and moulded largely by Rome. Persian influence was much stronger in the Christian border cultures of Georgia and Armenia, although here too the influence of Byzantium and, therefore, of Greece was paramount. Greek was probably both the official and the spoken language of most of the inhabitants who were not Georgians, Armenians or Kurds. We could thus call these people Anatolian Greeks, if we think of their language, or Eastern Orthodox Christians, if we consider their religion, which was then and for many centuries later, the real basis of their national and personal identity. Their racial origin need not concern us here. Clearly all the peoples that had inhabited Asia Minor – Hittites, Phrygians, Lydians, Galatians, Cappadocians, Carians and the rest, as well as those that had invaded the peninsula – had left their traces in the racial make-up of Anatolian Greeks. Since the peninsula had never been completely depopulated and then re-settled, some racial continuity must be assumed, in spite of periodic additions of invaders and immigrants. There must also have been some cultural continuity, the product not only of inherited tradition but also of a common environment. But having said that, we can surely forget the Hittites and the rest, at least as far as the history of Turkey is concerned, for when the Turks arrived on the scene not only the pre-Hellenic, but even the pre-Roman inhabitants of Asia Minor had ceased to live even in folk-memory.

Asia Minor does not seem to have been a very populous or prosperous area just before the Turkish conquest. It had been fought over almost continuously during the three preceding centuries. Great cities such as Amorium had been abandoned; others, such as Ephesus, were a shadow of their former selves. The ease with which Arabs had crossed the peninsula from end to end in the first century of Islam, the ease also with which room was found for large numbers of Turkish settlers after 1071, suggests that much of that vast land and particularly the Anatolian uplands had lain empty.

Who were the Turks, and where did they come from? There are many Turkish and also some non-Turkish historians who consider as Turks all people whose origin can be traced to Central Asia, Siberia and the great northern plains on either side of the Ural mountains and who speak agglutinative languages – languages in which the main roots of words remain unaltered, refinements of meaning being achieved by the addition of suffixes. If this definition is accepted Finns, Esthonians and Hungarians in the West and Mongols in the East (not to mention Huns and other extinct peoples) are all Turks. But of course they do not consider themselves Turks. People who call and have called themselves Turks came from across the eastern frontiers of the Islamic Caliphate in Central Asia, where they had lived mainly as nomads organized in tribes; they penetrated the Muslim Middle East first as mercenaries of the Abbasid Caliphs in the ninth century; they entered the Middle East already as Muslims, having been converted in their homeland by Arab and Persian missionaries, and they spoke a language recognizably akin to that spoken in Turkey today.

Among the many tribes of Turks the Oğuz, or Ghuzz as the Arabs called them, are the ancestors of the Turks in Turkey, as of the Azerbaijanis in the Soviet Union and Persia and of the Turkomans again in the Soviet Union, Persia, Turkey and elsewhere. The Oğuz Turks invaded and conquered most of the Islamic world in the tenth and eleventh centuries. They did so as Muslims. In 1055 an Oğuz Turk, Tughril-beg (or in modern Turkish spelling Tuğrul Bey), the founder of the Seljuk dynasty, entered Baghdad, the capital of the Islamic Caliphate, and had himself proclaimed Sultan, relegating the Caliph to a shadowy function. He came as the leader of large numbers of Oğuz Turks, and many of these war-like tribesmen pressed on westward to the frontiers of the Byzantine Empire, across which they proceeded to organize large-scale raids. They were not the first Turks or even the first Oğuz Turks to be seen there, for ever since the ninth century there had been Turks in the Muslim armies on the eastern frontier of Christendom. But this time they came in large numbers as Muslim Turkish conquerors, for already Islamic and Turkish were difficult to disentangle.

To the defenders of the Byzantine frontier these Turks were nomadic raiders, alien predators on a settled population. But they were also regarded as the spearhead of Islam, as warriors for the faith, as *ghazis*, to use the Arabic term universally understood and revered throughout Islam. They were assimilated to the existing tradition of frontier *ghazis*, and they gave this tradition a new lease of life. The Byzantine Emperor Romanos Diogenes made a supreme effort to defeat these swarms of Turkish raiders, of Muslim *ghazis*, and it was this effort that was crushed by the Turkish Seljuk Sultan Alparslan at the battle of Malazgirt in eastern Turkey in 1071. What the Muslim Turks crushed, in effect, was a motley array of mercenaries, an army which itself included some Turkish tribesmen. The battle of Malazgirt won the uplands of Asia Minor for the Turks, and it won them irrevocably. At first the Seljuks penetrated beyond the uplands to the westernmost limits of the peninsula, to the port of Smyrna (Izmir) on the Aegean Sea, or to Nicaea (Iznik in Türkish), not far from Constantinople itself. It was in Nicaea that the Seljuk prince Süleyman established his first capital in the land of Rum, in the territory, that is, won by Islam from the Eastern Roman Empire.

But the westernmost gains of the Seljuks were soon lost back to Christendom – to the Byzantine Greeks and to the Latins who came to rescue the Greeks as well as to serve their own interests. In 1134 the capital of the Seljuks of Asia Minor was transferred to Konya (ancient Iconium) in the centre of the Anatolian plateau, and except in the south, where the Seljuks held the Mediterranean coast of Asia Minor, it was, roughly speaking, the border between the plateau and the coastal plains that became the frontier between Islam and Christendom, between Turks on the one hand, and Greeks and Latins on the other.

Some time after the Seljuk conquest – how soon we do not know, but it was surprisingly soon – the Anatolian plateau became a Muslim Turkish land. There was a large influx of Turkish tribesmen, many of whom settled, giving their tribal names to hundreds of villages which can still be traced today on a map of Turkey. Many more remained nomads. These were the Turkomans, whose settlement is still not quite complete today. There were certainly conversions to Islam; there was also intermarriage, for Muslim canon law allowed Muslim men to take Christian or Jewish wives, although Muslim women could only take Muslims for husbands. The original local inhabitants of the Anatolian plateau were, however, allowed to keep their faith and to live on within the Muslim commonwealth as protected, but decidedly second-class citizens. Although there was no genocide of local Greeks or Armenians (it also appears that they did not leave the country in large numbers) non-Muslims soon became a minority in Asia Minor, and it was as a minority that they stayed for centuries in the land of their ancestors, until finally displaced in the upheavals of the First World War. They remained, until then, distinguished by their faith as Greek or Armenian Christians, but usually not by their language, for they gradually adopted the tongue of their Turkish neighbours. Such was the measure of the change of Asia Minor into a Turkish land, a change which followed with surprising rapidity the Turkish victory at Malazgirt in 1071.

Economically, the conquest of Asia Minor by Turkish tribesmen brought prosperity to the land. This seems paradoxical. One explanation is that Asia Minor profited from being joined to the rich world of Islam to the east, to Mesopotamia, Persia and Central Asia, just as it profited from ceasing to be an embattled frontier zone, which it had been during the preceding centuries of Byzantine rule. Perhaps it profited also from being governed under the *sharia*, the Holy Law of Islam, a law now often decried and universally fallen into disuse, but which for centuries had made for good and orderly government. It protected the persons and property of non-Muslims (provided, however, they submitted to Muslim rule), defined and limited taxes, allowed the setting up and upkeep of pious foundations and charities and regulated the orderly use and inheritance of property.

Whatever the causes, Seljuk rule saw a flowering of urban civilization in Asia Minor. Konya (Iconium), Sivas (Sebaste), Kayseri (Caesarea), Erzurum, Erzincan, Divriği and a host of other cities became prosperous centres of trade and culture, complete with mosques, bazaars, Coranic schools and colleges (*medrese*), hospitals, caravanserais, bath-houses and fountains. Many of these buildings have survived and are still the chief ornaments of their cities – witnesses to the golden age of the uplands of Asia Minor. Seljuk civilization was essentially Islamic, but it had an individual character. In Seljuk Asia Minor the language of scholarship was Arabic, that of literature and often of administration, Persian. The architecture of Seljuk monuments owed much to that of Persia and, also, since the Seljuk centre of gravity was in the east and north-east of the peninsula, to the styles of Georgia and Armenia.

Most of the people spoke Turkish, and in one Seljuk principality, that of Karaman in the Taurus mountains, Turkish was the official language. The Turks had, of course, also their own folk poetry and, some would claim, their own distinctive brand of Islam. Certainly it was not the *ulema*, the official expounders of Muslim orthodoxy, but dervishes, belonging to various mystical orders, often professing heretical opinions, who were most usually the mentors of the Turks in Asia Minor and particularly of the nomads amongst them. Many of these dervishes are known to have come from the old Turkish lands of Central Asia. It was they who inspired the Turks to battle, who were the agents of Turkish colonization, who wrote the Turks' poetry, around whose graves communities grew up. But dervish brotherhoods were a socially cohesive force in other non-Turkish Muslim lands as well, and perhaps we need not agree completely with some Turkish scholars and assume either an abiding Turkish inclination to heterodoxy, or a lack of conviction, in the Turks' own conversion to Islam. On the contrary, it was as the champions of official, orthodox Islam that the Turks achieved their greatest glory from the time of the Seljuks onwards. However, dervishes were always active amongst them and it is to their zeal that Seljuk and later Ottoman Turks owed many of their achieve-ments. So whether these dervishes were the descendants of *shamans*, the Turkish medicine-men of pagan times, or whether they were an Islamic phenomenon, they did colour Turkish Islam, even where they did not push it into heterodox paths.

In the middle of the thirteenth century, one hundred and seventy years after the battle of Malazgirt, the Seljuks of Asia Minor were over-whelmed by another wave of invaders from the East. The Mongols became the overlords of the Seljuk princes. They destroyed the central authority of the sultans of Konya, but they did not destroy the Turkish Muslim civilization of Asia Minor. On the contrary, some of the Anatolian cities, particularly those lying in the eastern part of the country, saw their prosperity increase under the Mongols. The two great saints of Muslim Anatolia – the mystic poet Jalaluddin Rumi, founder of the Mevlevi or whirling dervishes, and Hajji Bektash, the founder of another great order, that of the Bektashis (which was later to be associated with the Janissaries) – lived through the invasion and flourished after it. But one can go further and say that the Mongol invasion stimulated the second great wave of Turkish advance – an advance which started on the western edges of the Anatolian uplands and which was destined to take the Turks as far as the walls of Vienna.

There were two main reasons for this. The first was that the Mongol invasion brought large numbers of Turks into Anatolia. Some had been displaced by the Mongols, others accompanied them. At the end of the thirteenth century there were many more Turks in Asia Minor than there had been at the height of the power of the Seljuk sultans of Konya. There was thus a vast building-up of forces for a new assault on Christendom. The second reason lay in the very weakening of the authority of the sultans. They could no longer control the borders of Islam, which were taken over by a number of virtually independent warlords, leaders of *ghazis* whose reputation and whose livelihood depended on the prosecution of the Holy War against the infidel. Assured of independent action, assured also of enough men, since religious zealots, displaced tribesmen and soldiers of fortune from all over the Islamic world streamed to its westernmost frontier, these warlords went out not just to raid, but to conquer and settle the coastal plains of Asia Minor. The advance started at the end of the thirteenth century; fifty years later virtually the whole of Asia Minor was Turkish. In fact most of the land which we know as Turkey today had become Turkish and was becoming known as such to the West by the beginning of the fourteenth century. Some of it had been raided and briefly occupied by Seljuk Turks as early as the eleventh century, but it was now, after the Mongol invasion and through the agency of the *ghazi* princes, that the Anatolian coast became finally and irrevocably Turkish and Muslim.

History has preserved the names of most of the *ghazi* princes: Germiyan, Menteshe, Sarukhan, Aydın-oghlu and Osman – the son of Ertughrul, the father of Orkhan, the founder of the Ottoman dynasty. Osman's principality was on the north-western frontier, the frontier nearest the Byzantine capital, Constantinople. It was on the edges of the rich Bithynian plain. This was also the best defended Byzantine frontier – with the fortresses of Proussa, Nicaea and Nicomedeia guarding it from the east. Proussa (Bursa in Turkish) fell to Orkhan in 1326, some twenty years after his father, Osman, had first attacked it, and for the next three-quarters of a century it served as the capital of the Ottoman state.[3] By the time Bursa fell almost the whole of the Aegean coastal plain of Turkey had been reduced by other *ghazi* princes. Was it because the Ottomans were the last to arise that they were the longest to survive? Or was it because of the quality of their first sultans or the strategic importance of the area they occupied? Whatever the cause, as they pushed back the Byzantines, so too they extended their domains at the expense of their Turkish neighbours. By the end of the fourteenth century that second process was virtually completed and western Asia Minor, Turkish for a century already, had become an Ottoman possession. But by then the Ottoman Turks were victorious in Europe. There too they had been briefly preceded by other Turkish *ghazis* who had come to raid. The Ottomans came to conquer.

But before we look briefly at Turkish gains – and subsequent losses – in Europe, let us consider the completion and the consequences of their conquest of Asia Minor. Here too – as in the Anatolian uplands a couple of centuries earlier – they brought new prosperity. Rich Muslim cities sprang up: Ayasolug (among the ruins of Ephesus), Aydın, Manisa, Balıkesir, above all Bursa, where at the end of the fourteenth century one Western traveller saw two hundred thousand houses, eight hospitals 'where poor people are received, whether they be Christians, infidels or Jews' and many magnificent mosques.[4] In Bursa, as in other Anatolian towns, the original Greek inhabitants were driven out of their houses inside the city castle. But outside it – in the suburbs as well as the surrounding countryside – they were not only not molested but often encouraged to settle in order to man essential trades. However, they were almost from the start outnumbered by Muslim Turks. Converts from Greek and Armenian churches and, very occasionally, from Latin Christianity; Arabs and Persians (as scholars, divines, merchants or artisans); men of other Muslim countries attracted by new opportunities in these newly won lands, all came, swelling the number of Turks and diversifying their racial make-up. Gradually the type (or rather the types) of urban Turks was emerging, a type that looks more Mediterranean than Asian. However, it was the spirit that counted, and the spirit of this new people was Islamic.

In the cities the chief institution moulding life into an Islamic pattern was the *vakf*, or pious foundation. Public and private benefactors set up these foundations for the upkeep of mosques, schools, hospitals and other charities. The foundations could own land, shops, even whole bazaars, bath-houses, inns, etc. They employed many of the citizens. They pervaded the city, inspiring it with the aims of their founders, integrating it within the Islamic community. There were other institutions – dervish-houses, craft guilds – which served the citizens, but always with reference to the interests of the faith.

In spite of the constant wars which accompanied the advance of the Ottomans, many Anatolian Turkish cities carried on a profitable trade with Catholic Europe – Bursa in silk, the west Anatolian cities in grains and minerals, as well as in textiles. The Turkish conquest did not throw up a barrier round Asia Minor. On the contrary, as the prosperity of the area increased so trade with it grew. Culturally the area was joined to the Muslim world lying to the east of it; economically it preserved and even developed links with the West in addition to new ones which now stretched eastwards. Before the appearance of the Turks along the eastern seaboard of the Mediterranean, merchants, agents and whole colonies of the Italian city-states had become established in Byzantine territory. Ever since the Fourth Crusade, and in spite of the revival of Byzantine independence under the Palaeologi, Latin Christendom was paramount both politically and commercially in most of the lands of Byzantine culture. When the Turks resumed their advance westwards in the middle of the thirteenth century, it was the Latins rather than the Greeks who were their main foes. To divide the Greeks from the Latins became their abiding policy, and one that was by-and-large successful until modern times. Nevertheless, in spite of Turkish-Latin antagonism, Italian merchants continued visiting and often residing in the lands won by the Turks. We see them in the *ghazi* principalities of western Turkey in the fourteenth century. We see them – their ranks swollen by Frenchmen, Englishmen and Dutchmen – throughout subsequent centuries of Ottoman rule. Later, Jews acted as local intermediaries in the Levant trade; later still, they were largely superseded by Oriental Christians with whom Christian merchants in the West preferred to deal. But until modern times a Muslim Turkish merchant dealing with the West remained a rarity.

In 1352 the Ottoman Turks crossed into Europe and soon made themselves masters of the castle of Gallipoli. Ten years later the Sultan Murad I occupied Adrianople (Edirne) and proceeded to make it the capital of his empire. Fifty years later the Turks were already masters of the Balkan peninsula, most of which they were destined to hold for five centuries. They had beaten the Serbs, the Bulgarians and the Rumanians (Wallachians); at Nicopolis (Niğbolu) on the Danube in 1396 they crushed a great crusade in which almost the whole of Western Christendom had taken part. Only Constantinople remained to be reduced. A civil war in Islam – and among the Turks – gave it a reprieve of fifty years, for in 1402 the Ottoman Sultan Bayezid I was defeated near Ankara by Tamerlane (Timur Leng). Unlike the first great Mongol *khans*, Tamerlane was a Muslim; although he fought Muslims more often than Christians, he aspired to the title of *ghazi*, warrior for Islam. He was not so much a threat to Islam, as a champion of its eastern – in a way its more Turkish – half as against its western frontiersmen. He was successful in battle but, for a variety of reasons, of which distance and geography were not the least, the supremacy of Samarkand over the world of Islam could not be sustained. To Tamerlane, the Ottoman Sultan was one frontier *ghazi* prince among many; and after his victory, at Ankara, he proceeded to re-establish the *ghazi* principalities of Anatolia which the Ottomans had annexed.

But the frontier had moved west into Europe, and with it the designation Land of Rum, Rumeli, was transferred from Asia Minor to the Balkans. Whoever was lord of the frontier, and of the great

Muslim forces gathered there to fight the Christians, was the strongest prince in Islam. So it was from Adrianople that the Ottomans proceeded to reunify Asia Minor under their rule. And so strong were they, that while they did so, they extended their conquests in Europe and beat back the counter-attacks of Western Christendom. In 1444 a second great Crusade, led by the Hungarian champion John Hunyadi was defeated at Varna, not far from the Ottoman capital of Adrianople, by Sultan Murad II. Varna sealed the fate of Constantinople. The declining capital of the Byzantine Empire – which had become a city of ruins and of waste land inside its great walls – fell in 1453 to Murad's son, Mehmed II the Conqueror. The miracle of renascence, earlier seen in Erzurum, Konya and Bursa, was accomplished on a much larger scale when Constantinople became Istanbul. Its tiny population had all but perished or been exiled at the time of the conquest. Twenty years later there were already 16,000 families in the city, say 80,000 people, well over half of whom were Turks. By the middle of the sixteenth century the population had reached half a million, by the end of a century it was nearer a million.

Once again the city filled in the empty spaces within the walls. Once again mosques, standing at the centre of a network of schools, shops, bath-houses and inns, gave shape to a new community. Among these mosques the converted church of Santa Sophia was one of the richest and best-endowed. Where at first, after the conquest, Muslims and non-Muslims had to be drafted into the new capital, soon new settlers poured in from all over the Empire, a title which could now be applied to the Ottoman state without any qualification.

After the conquest of Constantinople Mehmed II claimed all the lands that had once been Byzantine. This claim he and his successors fully realized, even going beyond the frontiers of the Eastern Roman Empire at their furthest points. But in most lands where the Ottomans penetrated, the Byzantines had been there before. Even in Otranto in Italy, which Mehmed II conquered for a brief time, or along the North African coast, over which the Ottomans established a tenuous suzerainty in the sixteenth century, they had been preceded by the armies of Justinian. Gradually the Empire filled out: Mehmed II conquered the Peloponnese in the west, and the last remaining Christian enclave in

Asia Minor, the Kingdom of Pontus centred on the Black Sea port of Trebizond (Traubzon). Also in Asia Minor, he annexed the principality of Karaman in the Taurus mountains. His successor, Bayezid II, inflicted a first defeat on Venice and established the Ottoman Empire as a great naval power in the Mediterranean. Then Selim I, surnamed the Grim, defeated the Shiite Turkomans (who had conquered and were destined to mould the modern Persian Empire) and after establishing Ottoman rule in what is today eastern Turkey, penetrated into the Caspian basin – into towns that were to revert to Persia when, after much toandfroing, the frontier between the two countries assumed more or less its present shape in 1639. In the south Selim I defeated first the northern tribal allies of the Mamluks in lands that are now part of southern Turkey and then the Mamluks themselves, and annexed the Arab Near East and Egypt. Under Süleyman I, known as the Magnificent in the West and the Lawgiver in Turkey, first Rhodes then Belgrade fell to the Turks – and after Belgrade the whole of Hungary up to the gates of Vienna.

But the Ottomans were now reaching the boundaries of their ultimate expansion – Vienna eluded them and so did Malta. Nevertheless, Süleyman's successor Selim II could still extend the Empire by adding Cyprus to it. Then after half a century of decline and internal troubles, the Ottomans braced themselves for one last great effort. In 1669 they conquered Crete. It was a pyrrhic victory, and decline, this time irrevocable, set in almost immediately afterwards. In 1699 Austria recovered Hungary, but it was Russia that was to prove the Ottoman Empire's gravedigger in Europe. Still, in spite of Russia's growing strength and of Ottoman internal troubles, two more centuries had to pass before the Turks lost most of their European possessions. The defeat of the Turkish Empire was slowed down by rivalry between the Christian Great Powers, but Turkish courage and resilience also played a considerable part in averting an early rout.

2   The Ottoman background

THE OTTOMAN EMPIRE was the immediate precursor of the modern Turkish Republic. The Republic was built among its ruins; developed against its background. Modern Turkey is unintelligible unless one knows something of the character and the institutions which had made the Empire great and which then failed to prevent its collapse, a failure that was only aggravated by successive attempts to reform them.

The Ottoman Empire rose to greatness as a feudal, corporative, multi-national state integrated within the Holy Law of Islam. It was not an autocracy; even less was it a totalitarian state. It rested on delegated authority, on a balance of autonomous forces, groups and institutions. This nice balance was known as justice, in the traditional Muslim definition of justice as the mean between opposing forces. And justice, according to Muslim tradition, is the foundation on which a kingdom is built. But let us take these characteristics one by one.

Ottoman feudalism was based on the assumption that all conquered land — or as nearly all of it as makes no difference — belonged to the sovereign, who then granted the right to use it in return for obligatory military service. This right could be individual or hereditary; it could be more or less qualified. But the basis of the system was always that the feudal lord had to produce himself and his retinue to serve the sultan in time of war. In time of peace he was a resident landlord with a stake and a financial interest in the prosperity of his fief. Although he could be and often was a local tyrant, his tyranny was limited by the Holy Law. At least in theory, taxes could not be arbitrarily fixed: the Muslims' tithes and the non-Muslims' capitation tax were, again in theory, immutably fixed. The law also forbade compulsory labour. No doubt the provisions of the *sharia* were often violated and even more often circumvented, but at least at first, the law did provide a consider, able measure of protection to Ottoman subjects.

In addition to feudal levies, in addition also to tribal forces, the sultan also had his own army, which was in law a slave force. However the title 'Slave of the Porte', that is, of the palace, procured considerable advantages and was, therefore, often a matter of pride. The best,known element in that force was the Janissaries. The Janissaries were recruited from local non,Muslims whose boys were forcibly levied, converted to Islam and specially trained for the force. While slave troops had been used extensively by Muslim princes throughout the Middle Ages, this particular method of recruitment was an Ottoman and a canonical innovation. Its use was justified on the grounds that a Muslim com, mander was entitled to both human and physical booty when he triumphed over the infidels in the field. That the right to booty could become an abiding one, generations after the original resistance had been broken, was, of course, a legal fiction.

Christian observers were impressed by the fact that in order to put an army in the field (in order to mobilize his feudal levies and to despatch his Janissaries) the Ottoman sultan did not have to consult a Diet, that he did not have to convince refractory burghers. They therefore thought him an autocrat. But the sultan was free to act only within the provisions of the *sharia* or to the extent to which he could twist the *sharia* to suit his purposes. He was certainly not above the law. He was the guardian of it, and he could be deposed for infringing it. This was in fact the standard justification for deposing sultans, even where their overthrow had little to do with law,keeping or law,breaking. The ruling institu, tion was not the monarchy but Islam, whose interests were served by two main classes – the scholars, that is, the interpreters of the law, judges, bureaucrats and clerks, and the soldiers, in the first place the Slaves of the Porte. These institutions had their chief officers: the Commander or Agha of the Janissaries, the military commanders *beylerbeyi* (literally lords of feudal lords) of Roumelia (Turkey,in,Europe) and Anatolia (Turkey,in,Asia); the Shaykh al,Islam or Chief Mufti; the chief military judges (*Kadı al,asker*). Outside the ruling institution itself, corporate organizations abounded: the various groups of non-Muslims had their communal organizations known as *millet*, under their Patriarchs or Chief Rabbi; the guilds had their officers, and so down to every tribe with its *shaykh* and village with its headman. Each officer was responsible for the good behaviour of the members of the organization over which he presided; each enjoyed considerable delegated authority, which he exercised at great personal risk if his subordinates caused trouble. But then the sultan himself was by no means immune from danger if he allowed the balance of forces within his realm to be upset.

This was the system by which the Ottoman Empire grew strong. Then at the end of the seventeenth century things went radically and irrevocably wrong. Contemporary Turkish commentators saw and defined the disease in terms with which they were familiar: they saw that the organs of the state had ceased to perform the functions assigned to them; that the balance between them had been disturbed. This added up to the Muslim definition of injustice. They often ascribed this injustice to sin, to wilful disregard of the law. Certainly the spirit seemed to go out of a body which the *sharia* had held together and inspired. But there were, of course, more mundane causes: the Empire was over-extended; its military efforts had outrun its reserves – and so currency was devalued, taxes raised, offices sold. Military fief-holders gave way to absentee landlords and tax-farmers. As the central government tried to extract more resources, oppression and injustice travelled down the whole system. It is thus true that the failure was economic, but it is equally true that political miscalculation in the prosecution of campaigns and personal faults in leadership produced economic failure. There were inherent disadvantages in the system: it was essentially medieval, pre-technological, excessively conservative: it was collectivist in an age that was gradually groping its way towards individualism.

Other unfavourable developments were outside control: the rising prosperity of Western Europe and the increasing strength of Russia tilted the balance of power in favour of Christendom. And as the attraction of the Christian powers increased, as the benefits of Ottoman rule became more and more problematical, so the loyalty of the

Christian subjects of the Empire began to waver. This process was slower than was at first realized: in the seventeenth century Russian agents trying to subvert the Greeks had to promise that they would treat them at least as well as the Turks had done.[5] But the decline of religion dealt Ottoman power its worst blow – where Eastern Orthodox Christianity had refused to cooperate with the Catholic West, Levantine nationalists could and did gather under the religiously neutral banner of freedom, progress and nationalism which the West raised in the Age of Enlightenment. True, religious dissension among Christians (between Greek Orthodox and Catholics and between Catholics and Protestants) from which the Ottoman Empire had profited for centuries, was to some extent replaced by rivalry among the Great Powers, and the Ottomans profited from that too insofar as they could. However, in spite of their rivalry, the European Great Powers did on the whole support nationalistic risings within the Ottoman Empire. It was this support which gave Greece its independence. Nevertheless, Great Power politics also worked in favour of the Turks – as when the Congress of Berlin postponed the dismemberment of Turkey-in-Europe. By that time the 'sick man' of Europe was on his deathbed. As in the case of other multi-national empires in modern times, it was nationalism which proved the agent of the final break-up, but in the case of the Ottoman Empire the rise of nationalism had been preceded by at least a century by the Empire's own failure – military, economic and moral.

The Empire did not fall either without a military struggle or without attempts at internal reform. The military struggle – particularly the series of wars with Russia and finally the world war – was a spirited and often heroic rear-guard action which failed. The reforms failed too. This failure must be defined and, if possible, explained.

There are two distinctly different failures with which the rulers of the Ottoman Empire are reproached. The first is usually defined as a failure to westernize their country – to develop the country in the manner and to the level achieved in the West. The second is simply a failure to preserve the Empire. However, although economic underdevelopment may have helped in the break-up of the Ottoman Empire, these two failures are not essentially connected. Economic backwardness did not cause the break-up of the Austro-Hungarian or, for that matter, of the

British Empire. If the Ottoman Empire went the way of all multi-national empires (with the exception of the Russian one) and broke apart, it was not through lack of westernization, but because the Western ideology of nationalism had subverted its subjects. Nationalists among the subject peoples, and their sympathizers in the West, complained loudly of 'Oriental maladministration' in the Ottoman Empire, but reforms only served to encourage their efforts to break loose. The more freedom they gained, the more they used that freedom to carve for themselves separate national states. Furthermore, Russia, the Ottoman's main foe, was not interested in a reformed Ottoman Empire. So the promulgation of the first Ottoman Constitution in 1876 was immediately followed by a Russian onslaught. So too the Young Turkish Revolution of 1908 was followed by the formal annexation of Bosnia and Herzegovina by Austro-Hungary; then by the Italian attack on Tripolitania in 1911 and finally, in the following year, by the united attack on the Empire by the Balkan States which wrested from it all its European possessions up to and including the city of Adrianople (Edirne).

Ottoman internal reforms were powerless to avert this consummation. The first serious attempt at reform was made by Sultan Selim III in the closing years of the eighteenth century. However, Selim III's New Army, a body independent of the Janissaries, was short-lived. In 1807 a popular revolt put an end to Selim III and his reforms. In 1826, in the middle of the Greek War of Independence, Sultan Mahmud II dramatically broke the old order by destroying the Corps of Janissaries. In so doing he may have followed Peter the Great of Russia's example who, a century earlier, had similarly destroyed the Corps of the Streltzi. The consequences of the two acts were, however, different. The Ottomans did in fact subdue the Greeks but the Great Powers intervened and forced them to concede independence to a small Greek State. It was an example that was to be followed later, when Ottoman victories over Serbs and Montenegrins were invariably set at nought by Western intervention. The reforms continued and in 1839 Mahmud's son, Sultan Abdul Mejid, proclaimed the beginning of a new regime, called the Tanzimat, a new order guaranteeing equality to all Ottoman subjects and promising them the inviolability of their lives and property.

27

In 1856, the year in which the Crimean War ended, another Imperial Charter reinforced the guarantees of equal treatment given to non-Muslims, who were freed from the canonical capitation tax. (This was more or less replaced by payments made by non-Muslims in lieu of military service, a much politer form of taxation.) Then came the Constitution of 1876, which was followed by the election of the first Ottoman Parliament in 1877. After the defeat of the Ottomans at the hands of the Russians, the Ottoman Parliament was prorogued for an indefinite period by Sultan Abdul Hamid who believed that he could preserve his empire by more traditional means. Nevertheless the Constitution remained officially in force, and in 1908 Abdul Hamid was obliged by the Army to summon another Parliament. This military coup, which is known as the Young Turkish Revolution, was taken a step further in 1909 when Abdul Hamid was deposed after the failure of another conservative popular rising. Power thereafter rested more or less in the hands of the Young Turk revolutionary officers who, after the first disaster of the Balkan War in 1912, led the Empire to a second and final disaster in the First World War. In that war – in Gallipoli, Galicia, the Caucasus, Syria and Mesopotamia – the Turks fought as well as they had ever fought and although they could not save the Empire, they did save their homeland in the subsequent fighting against the Greeks which lasted until 1922, by which time Turkey had been at war for eleven years, almost without a break.

Although the century of pre-republican reforms did not save the Empire, important changes were made. The Ottoman ruling institution – the structure of the wielders of power – was transformed. The first beneficiary of the change was the sultan himself who came nearer to the traditional Western image of an autocrat. Freed of the menace of the Janissaries and then little by little of the trammels of the Holy Law, he gained greater freedom to fashion the new order. Traditional corporate organizations lost their autonomy. The *ulema*, the Muslim Canon lawyers who were at once judges, bureaucrats and teachers, were driven from the bureaucracy, then from education (or rather the most important part of it) and from the judiciary. Towards the end of the Empire they counted for little. Their schools had become seminaries, their tribunals consistory courts, their canonical judgments an unimportant formality.

In the provinces, autonomous *pashas*, feudal lords and notables were largely suppressed or annexed to the bureaucracy. Tribes were brought under closer control, settled or bought as military auxiliaries. A serious attempt was made to put the whole country into a straitjacket of bureaucratic centralism. But the board was not swept clean; the social configuration of the country was too strong for it. However, enough was swept away to make the new bureaucracy and above all, the army, supreme. In the West absolutism was a bridge between feudalism and democracy. In the Ottoman Empire absolutism was replaced in power by an alliance of the army and of the civil service.

This was the main social process that accompanied the disintegration of the Ottoman Empire from the Greek War of Independence to the First World War, that is, from 1826 to 1918. Among Muslims it encountered remarkably little resistance, partly because the abrogation of the Holy Law, and of the social order which it sustained, was carried out in the name of the Holy Law, partly because the sultan was instinctively trusted by the Muslims as the Commander of the Faithful, and the Guardian of the Community of Islam; largely also because the Janissaries who could depose a reforming sultan in 1807, were, as we have seen, destroyed in 1826, and reaction was left unarmed. Pretences were kept up: the Tanzimat Charter was officially a revival of the Holy Law; the Constitution an embodiment of the Coranic precept of consultation among the faithful, while the soldiers who were despatched to Istanbul in 1909 to depose Sultan Abdul Hamid were told that they were marching to free the sovereign's person from constraint. Through-out the period, the Muslims reacted by attacking non-Muslims, by so-called massacres. This was not only because the new order was felt to be an infidel order, it was because the infidels were seen or believed to be doing well at the expense of Islam. They were encroaching from within and without, and the Muslims hit back instinctively. Those who hit back most savagely were the wild men amongst them – Albanian, Circassian, Kurdish and Druze tribesmen.

The Ottoman Empire, as we have seen, was a multi-national empire and the main line of division among its subjects was between Muslims and non-Muslims. The Muslims were in the majority in Asia, the non-Muslims in Europe. There was also this difference: that while in

Asia Minor not only most Muslim but also non-Muslims spoke Turkish, in the Balkans most Muslims spoke local languages – Serbo-Croat, Albanian, Bulgarian and Greek. When Christian states were formed in the Balkans, the Muslims, whatever their language, suffered equally: some were killed, many expelled, many more migrated to lands which remained under Ottoman rule. There was a similar movement of Muslims from the north, from lands conquered by Russia; 700,000 Circassians are said to have migrated to Turkey in 1864.[6] Some were settled in Bulgaria, where they seem to have been largely responsible for the massacres of Bulgarians in subsequent years, others in Arab lands, but most in Asia Minor. There were Abkhazes also from the Caucasus, Tartars from the Crimea and refugees from other Muslim peoples and tribes. In the Balkans, as frontiers were rolled back, so refugees came rolling in. Nevertheless, after the Congress of Berlin in 1878 there were already large numbers of Muslims outside the frontiers of the Ottoman Empire: those in Austria-Hungary were largely Serbo-Croat-speaking Bosnians, but in Rumania and particularly in Bulgaria there were large numbers of Turks – probably over a million. On the other hand, in the remaining Ottoman possessions in Europe – in Albania and Macedonia – there were many Christians. Again we do not know how many, but in Macedonia there was certainly a preponderance of Christians, most of them Slavs, although Muslims accounted for thirty to forty per cent of the population. Most of these were Albanians, the number of Turkish-speaking Muslims in Macedonia being variously put at 250,000 to half a million.[7] It is from the frontier population of Turks that there came Mustafa Kemal Atatürk, the founder of the modern Turkish Republic. Generally speaking Macedonia in the west and the frontier garrison of Erzurum in the east were for the Turkish officer corps a fertile recruiting ground, as Alsace was for the French and Northern Ireland for the British armies.

Even after the Congress of Berlin the Turks identified completely with Islam. For a moment it looked as if the hard-pressed Muslim community might close its ranks, that a Muslim nationalism might be born. 'The Turks of the present day,' the British Ambassador in Istanbul, Sir William White, wrote to Lord Salisbury in 1889, 'appear more and more to look, not to Imperial, but to Mussulman interests, and to consider the Balkan peninsula as lost to them.'[8] This attempt to form a Muslim common front, to nurture, as it were, a spirit of Muslim nationalism (an ideal which, as Pakistan has shown, is perfectly feasible) was one of the main aims of Sultan Abdul Hamid, whose reign is invariably described by Turkish historians as one of the darkest tyranny and reaction. And certainly Muslim nationalism would have been a conservative force – as a religious rather than secular ideology. Abdul Hamid failed partly because the secularization of the Ottoman ruling class continued in his reign and was in fact accelerated by his own prodigious campaign of school-building. After Abdul Hamid was overthrown, the development of Muslim nationalism was foiled by a number of different factors – the centralizing policy of the Young Turks, which alienated Muslim Albanians as well as some Arabs; Albanian fears that Istanbul would sacrifice them to Balkan Christians; the emergence of Arab nationalism – compounded of the secessionist urges of Syrian Christians, of Bedouin tribalism and of Western promptings; and finally the birth of Turkish nationalism itself. This last phenomenon was a tardy growth which hardly showed above ground at the turn of the century. It took two further blows – the loss of the Balkans with its Albanians in 1912 and of the Arabs in 1918 – to make it seem the only tenable theory by which the Turks could explain their identity.

Nationalism is an aspect of westernization and it became the main ideology of the Ottoman ruling class of officers and bureaucrats, a class that was fairly thoroughly westernized under the reforming sultans. The other main group of people whom the reforms affected and benefited economically was that of non-Muslims – Greeks, Armenians, Jews and others. It is often said that the sultans' reforms failed where those of the Japanese Court succeeded – that they failed in grafting Western economy, technology and a Western technological society on an Oriental body. But in fact, if they failed among the Turks, they succeeded among the non-Muslims. The nineteenth century, particularly the second half of it, was an age of prosperity for Ottoman Greeks, Armenians, Christian Syrians and Jews. A French historian writing at the time of the Greek War of Independence, predicted that an independent Greece would act as a magnet for all the Greeks of the Ottoman Empire, which would languish without them.[9] In fact the opposite happened; Greeks from independent Greece sought the prosperity which Istanbul, Izmir (Smyrna) and the Aegean coast offered, once the sultans promised and started applying a measure of equality to Christians and non-Christians alike. They were joined there by Greeks from the interior of Asia Minor. Similarly it was the Age of the Tanzimat reforms that saw the rise to prosperity of Armenian communities outside historical Armenia – in Istanbul, Bursa, Izmir, Trabzon and in other cities. The Ottoman Empire under the reforming sultans, like Egypt under British protection, was a fertile field for the enterprise of local (as well as foreign) Christians and Jews. It is they who were westernized – socially and economically – and westernization stopped short at them. The Aegean coast was made prosperous by and for the Greeks, the Black Sea coast by and for the Greeks and Armenians. When they were driven out after the First World War and the Turkish War of Independence, economic development and westernization had to start all over again.

The mass of Turks in Asia Minor were as untouched by westernization as their country was innocent of economic development. As early as the seventeenth century, Asia Minor, bled white by the sultans' campaigns, fell into anarchy, its social fabric disrupted by rebellions and brigandage. In the succeeding centuries further wars completed the ruin, while reforms served only to destroy what traditional forces of social cohesion there had been. In 1881 a French writer gave this account of Asia Minor: 'There are districts where harvests are left to rot for lack of transport and because of the insecurity of the roads . . . Kurds, Bedouins . . . Circassians, refugees from all the countries lost by the Empire and driven to crime by misery, scour the roads at will . . . At the gates of Izmit (not far from the capital) market gardeners are robbed and murdered. There are even pirates in the Sea of Marmora and on the Bosporus!'[10]

This decadence of Muslim society, this contrast between the squalor of the mass of the Turks and the rising prosperity of the Christians, drove the latter to tempt Providence. Under the banner of nationalism they claimed territory where they were in the majority; appealing to history, they claimed lands that had once belonged to their real or presumed ancestors. In accordance with the two principles of majority rule and historic restitution the Turks, it seems, were to pass under alien rule everywhere – except perhaps the central steppe of Asia Minor. But the existence of Turks – of whom there must have been some ten million in the Ottoman Empire at the beginning of the First World War, could not be conjured away. The Christians of Asia Minor – or, more accurately, their nationalist leadership – overreached and destroyed themselves, and their destruction naturally led to the birth of a national Turkish republic.

The maps on pages 34 and 35 can give only an approximate idea of the ebb and flow of Ottoman power. Cities were captured, lost, then captured again. Boundaries shifted with changes in the power and influence not only of Sultans, but also of their provincial governors and vassals. The degree of Ottoman control over nominally subject tribes – in South Russia, the Caucasus, the Middle East and North Africa – varied from time to time, and the tribes themselves sometimes moved from place to place. When the Empire contracted, Ottoman power often faded out in stages: first real control was lost, except perhaps in the chief city of the province, then the loss of control was formally acknowledged. Sometimes the date of legal cession is itself ambiguous. Thus Britain occupied Cyprus in 1878 and annexed it unilaterally in 1914, but Turkey did not acknowledge the loss until 1923. Similarly the loss of Egypt can be dated 1799 (French occupation), 1805 (recognition of Muhammad Ali as autonomous Governor), 1831 (Muhammad Ali's revolt), 1841 (end of revolt), 1914 or even 1923. Finally, in the case of eastern Caucasus and Azerbaijan, only the dates of more or less effective Ottoman occupation can be given.

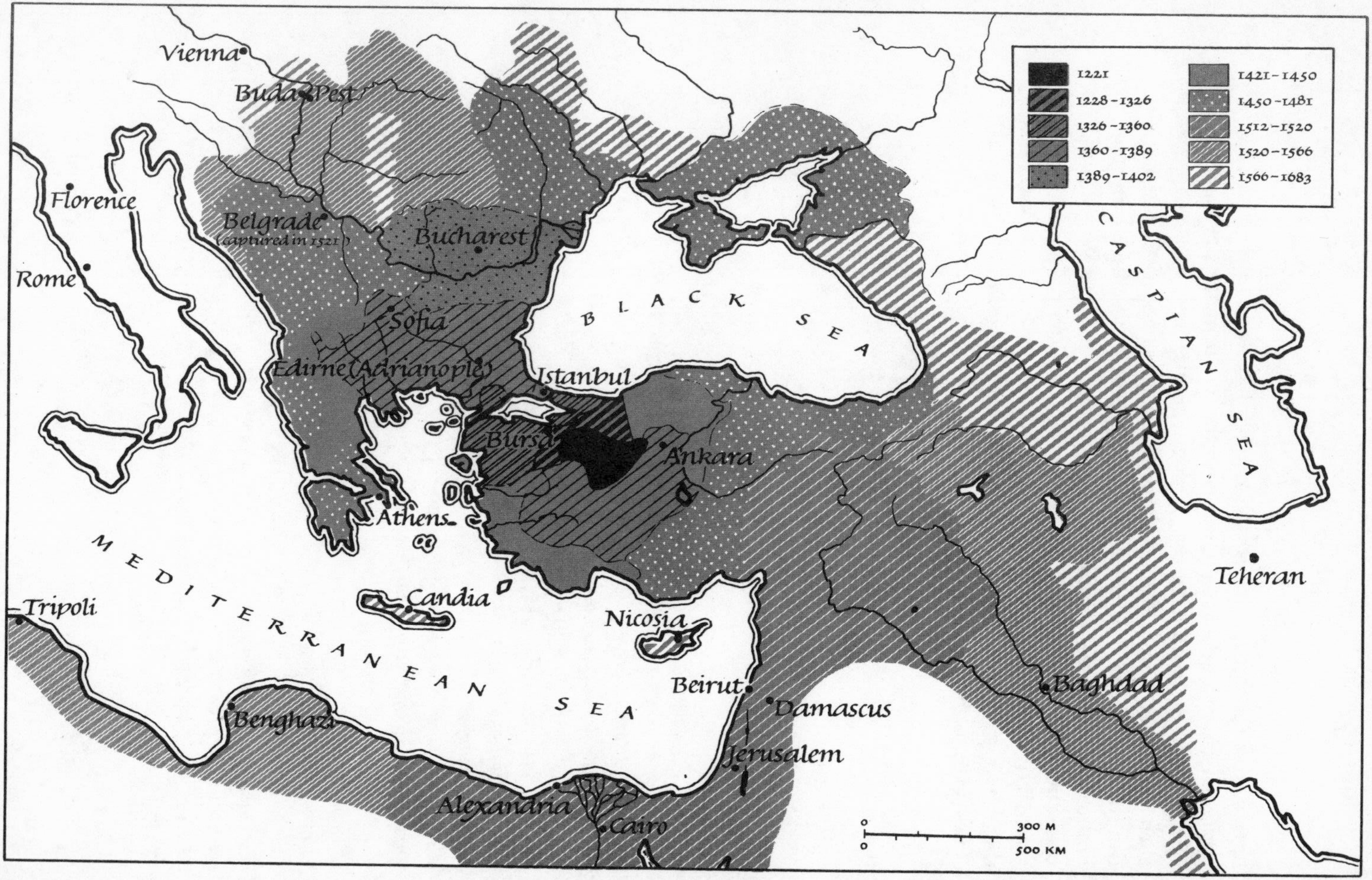

Legend:

1421–1450
1450–1481
1512–1520
1520–1566
1566–1683

1221
1228–1326
1326–1360
1360–1389
1389–1402

300 M
500 KM

CASPIAN SEA

Teheran

Baghdad

BLACK SEA

Damascus
Jerusalem
Beirut

Ankara

Istanbul

Nicosia

Bursa

MEDITERRANEAN SEA

Cairo

Alexandria

Candia

Athens

Edirne(Adrianople)

Sofia

Bucharest

Belgrade
(captured in 1521)

Budapest

Vienna

Florence

Rome

Tripoli

Benghazi

Expansion of the Ottoman Empire

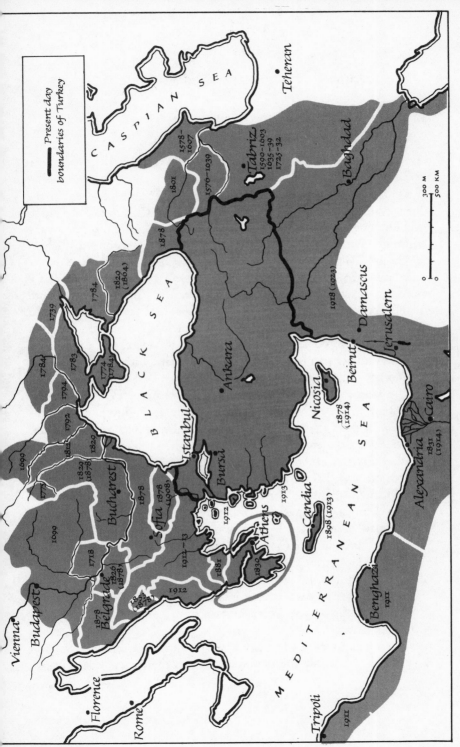

Contraction of the Ottoman Empire

3   Defeat and victory

THE MULTI-NATIONAL OTTOMAN EMPIRE perished in the
First World War. Under the leadership of the Committee of Union
and Progress (the Young Turks' official name), as expressed in the
triumvirate of Enver, Talat and Cemal Pashas, it entered the war
recklessly. To some extent it was even tricked into the war by the
Germans. However, it was natural for many Turks to believe that if
Russia, and after the Anglo-Franco-Russian Entente, Britain and
France too, were in one camp, they belonged to the other. The spirited
resistance put up by the Turks in the war in spite of every material
disadvantage – poor communications, a total lack of industry, a
military and civilian bureaucracy unable to cope with modern military
technology – could not avert their defeat.

The war itself produced demographic changes in Asia Minor.
Christians in the war zones – whose sympathy lay indubitably with the
enemies of the Ottoman state – were forcibly moved inland. These
moves, which were approved and possibly initiated by German
military advisers affected some Greeks along the Aegean and Black
Sea coasts, as well as the mass of Armenians on the Black Sea coast and
in the eastern uplands. Many (some say most) of the exiles perished –
through hunger, privation and the attacks of a local Muslim population
which had been stirred by stories of the oppression of Muslims in
Ottoman lands lost to Christians, and which felt itself at bay. The
Turks' own losses were immense – at the front as well as in the interior.
Among them, too, hunger and privation took a heavy toll, while the
Armenians themselves were not innocent of killing Turkish civilians
who fell in their power, when Russian troops moved inexorably into
Ottoman territory.

When the armistice was signed, the Ottoman government was still
in control of roughly the whole territory of the present-day Turkish

Republic. In Asia Minor there were at that time, according to Turkish statistics, some 9,300,000 Muslims (predominantly Turks) a million Greeks and just over half a million Armenians. In addition, in eastern Thrace – all that was left of Ottoman possessions in Europe, after the Balkan wars of 1912–13 – there had been in 1914, 360,000 Turks and 225,000 Greeks. Finally, in Istanbul there were over half a million Turks and just under a quarter of a million Greeks.[11] This whole territory was guarded by the remnants of the Ottoman armies, which numbered 640,000 men in 1914, but which, after sustaining heavy losses, and after a partial demobilization imposed by the victorious allies, were reduced by 1919 to little more than 50,000 men.[12] By far the largest remaining Ottoman force was the Army of the Caucasus, formed by the Young Turk leader Enver Pasha to carve a Great Turan – a state grouping all the Turkish-speaking peoples – out of the stunned body of the Czarist Empire. After the armistice, this army, renamed 15th Army Corps and placed under a new commander, Kâzım Karabekir Pasha, was concentrated near Erzurum.

The Ottoman leaders – the last Sultan, Mehmed Vahdettin, the pashas who assumed power under him after the fall of the Young Turks, and many, if not most, educated Turks – believed or professed to believe that President Wilson's principle of the self-determination of nations would be applied to the Ottoman Empire and that, therefore, the lands where the Muslims formed the majority of the population, and where, as we have seen, the writ of the Ottoman government still ran, were safe. They knew that Armenians, and, to a lesser extent, Greeks, who had suffered from deportations and massacres, were burning with revenge. They were prepared to sacrifice Young Turkish war criminals, but their remaining territory they hoped to keep. However, moral indignation on behalf of the oppressed Christians, greed, intrigues among the Great Powers and incitement by prospective successor states, as well as the spectacle of Ottoman helplessness – all these led the Allies to a half-hearted attempt to make a final division of the Ottoman Empire and deny the Turks the two supremely modern rights of self-determination and majority rule.

We can see today that even if this attempt had been determined and sustained, even if the Great Powers had been united internally and among themselves in a resolve to deny self-rule to the Turks (instead of harbouring pro-Turkish factions and politicians, who on occasion influenced their policies), even then the attempt would have failed. Now that we have seen the direct application of France's strength fail in its effort to suppress a force as recent and at first as puny-looking as Algerian nationalism, we are in a better position to realize the absurdity of the earlier attempt to suppress the Turks through the indirect agency of Greek and Armenian nationalism. But the absurdity was not evident at the time. Not only did the Allies expect their commands to be obeyed, but the Sultan and his advisers themselves failed to see how obedience could be withheld. The only weapon which they used and which they knew how to use was to try to stir up dissension among their adversaries. But this was a weapon of doubtful efficacy when there was enough booty lying around to satisfy everyone's greed. In any case, this is a weapon which can be used only when there is some means of resistance left. But the Sultan and his advisers believed that resistance was impossible, that docility alone (accompanied by a few fatuous underhand intrigues) could win concessions. This belief, which was shared by many Turks, as well as a lassitude which affected most of them, after the vicissitudes of the First World War, obscured the strength of the Turkish position. Once defeatism was dissipated, once a will to resist was born and then channelled into an effective organization, military victory over the Greeks and Armenians (for none was required over the Great Powers) proved surprisingly easy. According to official Turkish statistics, the Turkish national armies lost nine thousand men in campaigns which lasted over three years, campaigns which led to the defeat of the Greeks in the west and of the Armenians in the east. Nine thousand killed, 31,000 wounded (and 22,500 men but only 147 officers lost through disease) was the entire military human cost of forging a national Turkish state.[13] Compared with the losses suffered by the Ottoman armies in the First World War this was insignificant. The defence of Gallipoli alone had cost the Turks 55,000 killed, 100,000 wounded, 21,000 dead from disease and 10,000 missing, and the operations in eastern Anatolia against the Russians had been even more costly.[14] But although, seen in retrospect, the Turkish military victory in the War of Independence seems now pre-ordained, almost easy, what was not easy was to rouse the Turks to the effort which it required. Mustafa Kemal Pasha, the founder of the modern Turkish Republic, who later took the name Atatürk (meaning Father of the Turks), is rightly known as the begetter and the organizer of this effort, but it was the Allies who gave him his chance.

It is interesting, although perhaps unprofitable, to speculate on what would have happened if the Allies had been true to their professed principles, if they had told local Greeks and Armenians that they would have to settle down under the Turks who in spite of their defeat in the First World War, could not be deprived of lands where they formed the majority of the population. The Muslim inhabitants of present-day Turkey certainly wanted nothing better than to be given a chance to live in peace in their own country, and to live as their ancestors had done – only, if possible, more prosperously. By 1918 the eastern half of that country had been devastated, its male population decimated. There were widespread shortages, even famine. Banditry which had, in any case, been endemic in Anatolia, increased in scale and audacity as the professionals were joined by deserters and then by soldiers demobilized into destitution. In spite of all the efforts at unification and centralization made by Ottoman reformers over the preceding hundred years (and in some cases because of them), these remaining lands of the Ottoman Empire still retained their old, medieval, social diversity.

As a result of the reforms, the educated leadership became alienated from the mass of Muslims; as a result of the war, officers were disliked, sometimes hated, by the peasants whom they had led to defeat and death. The capital, Istanbul, which was governed separately and whose inhabitants had been almost until the last exempted from the obligation of military service, was detached in spirit and in way of life from Anatolia. Anatolia itself was by no means a social unit. The Turkish peasantry formed the homogeneous core of its population. But, apart from the Christian minorities, there were Circassians and Abkhazes with their own minority sub-cultures in the west, Kurdish tribesmen in the east, Lazes (a Muslim people related to the Georgians) in the north. There were quasi-autonomous religious orders – Nakshibendis among the Kurds, Mevlevis (whirling dervishes) and Bektashis among the Turks of central Anatolia. There were powerful local notables, feudal lords, heads of clans. The Muslim's allegiance was often to his *shaykh, bey, agha, baba* – local religious or secular notables bearing a variety of names and exercising a variety of powers. As the power of central government weakened, forces that had been held in check for over a century reappeared. The one real unifying link, the one source of personal commitment, was Islam, with the sultan as its traditional guardian. The ideology of Turkish nationalism had won a hold only over the educated and not over all of them. The 'National Covenant' promulgated by the last Ottoman Parliament as late as 17 February 1920, makes no mention of Turks, only of the 'Ottoman Muslim majority'. In Istanbul the Allies captured the minds and bodies of the official leaders of that majority, but, by putting the Turks in fear of their lives and property, they themselves mobilized against the promptings of official Islam, the promptings of fear and of the will to survive. In any case, there is no apostolic succession in Islam – the sultan can be deposed if he betrays his trust, the Shaykh al-Islam or Chief Mufti if he misinterprets the Holy Law. And, traditionally, it is the safety of the faithful, as well as the purity of the doctrine, which is the chief concern of the guardians of Islam. On 15 May 1919 when the Greeks, with Allied approval, landed in Izmir, the safety of Turkish Muslims was put in immediate and obvious danger. It was soon clear that Greek occupation, unlike the presence of the forces of the Allied Great Powers, was meant to be permanent, that the Allies really intended to carve up Turkey. The Sultan's government reacted verbally, the more warlike among the population took up arms. The Turkish War of Independence began and Mustafa Kemal Pasha had his chance to save and shape his country.

Mustafa Kemal created the Turkish Republic. He won its territory, chose and built its capital, shaped its institutions, devised its alphabet and even its language, set it on a road of his choosing. He stands apart as the father of modern Turkey. Yet he was also a representative Young Turk officer of his generation. What distinguished him was clear-sighted ability – the ability of an outstanding general and also of a successful civilian organizer. 'What is the secret of happiness?' he was asked in his later years. 'Success,' he replied, 'I am happy because I have been successful.' But if modern Turkey is the product of Mustafa

Kemal's genius, that genius was the embodiment of the aspirations of educated Turks of his background and generation.

Mustafa Kemal was born in Salonica in 1881, the son of a minor Ottoman civil servant. Like many other Turks of lower middle-class background he chose the army for his career. Like most cadets in the closing years of the reign of Sultan Abdul Hamid he was involved in mildly dangerous conspiratorial activities – which earned him a provincial posting after he was commissioned. In the provinces he could plot even more freely, particularly after he was transferred from Syria to Macedonia. Macedonia was full of discontented officers – discontented at the politics and the tactics of the unending war against Slav terrorists, unhappy also at the contrast between the inefficiency of their military organization and the inadequacy of their pay on the one hand, and the happy lot of foreign advisers, attached to the Ottoman army, on the other. Mustafa Kemal shared this discontent and was party to the conspiracy which led to the Young Turk *pronunciamento* of July 1908, but he does not seem to have played an important part in it. Less than a year later, when a counter-revolutionary mutiny broke out in Istanbul, he was already in the front rank of those who organized a military force to suppress it. Then, the ways of the Young Turk military leaders and those of Mustafa Kemal gradually began to part. Mustafa Kemal is usually said to have opposed the army's involvement in politics, which the Young Turks, as military politicians, allowed. The main difference, however, was one of approach and temperament. The Young Turk leaders – Enver, Talat, Cemal and the rest – were adventurers. Mustafa Kemal was not. He concentrated on his military career, on improving his professional qualifications. Turkey's entry into the Great War, of which he strongly disapproved, found him in Sofia as Ottoman military attaché.

It was, in fact, the Great War which gave Mustafa Kemal his first chance to prove himself. He was appointed Commander of the 19th Division in the Dardanelles area and it was his Division that faced the first British landing parties at Arıburnu on 25 April 1915. Here Mustafa Kemal rallied his troops and avoided a rout. His decisiveness is reflected in his first famous order: 'I don't order you to attack; I order you to die. During the time it takes us to die, other forces may come here to replace us.' Promoted Colonel, Mustafa Kemal was given command of the Anafartalar sector, where he launched a successful counter-offensive, which stabilized the front and thus led eventually to the British decision to call off the whole operation. It was his first success in Gallipoli which made Mustafa Kemal a popular hero and allowed him later to take undisputed command of all the Turkish national forces which resisted the envisaged partition of their country. Two more successes followed: as Commander of the 16th Army Corps on the front of the Caucasus, Mustafa Kemal, now a *pasha* or general, re-captured from the Russians the east Anatolian towns of Mus and Bitlis. The second success was less explicit, but more interesting. He was in command of the Seventh Ottoman Army facing Allenby in Palestine, when the Ottoman front was broken in an adjoining sector. It became Mustafa Kemal's task to save what could be saved. This he did, much better than is realized. He refused to fight for either Damascus or Aleppo and retreated headlong until he could regroup his forces on a line which more or less follows Turkey's southern frontier today. This ruthless ability to sacrifice territory in order to save his forces, disregarding both prestige and sentiment, stood Mustafa Kemal in good stead later in his campaign against the Greeks.

Just before the Ottoman Empire surrendered in October 1918, Mustafa Kemal, who had in the meantime been appointed to the command of all Ottoman forces on the Syrian front, felt himself important enough to ask the Sultan to appoint him Minister of War. The Sultan refused. Mustafa Kemal was also unable to sway the Ottoman politicians to his views, when he returned to Istanbul after the armistice. But among nationalist officers Mustafa Kemal's pre-eminence was undisputed. So when he failed in his efforts to get the Sultan's government to adopt a policy of resistance to the Allies he secured for himself the post of Inspector of the Third Army in Anatolia. This Army, which consisted largely of the units under the command of Kâzım Karabekir Pasha in Erzurum, was the last coherent Ottoman force which was left to be commanded or inspected; it was the only base of military resistance. Although the base was under the command of another general, Mustafa Kemal, instead of becoming the latter's protégé succeeded by force of personality as well as by the weight of his reputation in imposing his leadership both on Karabekir and, with much less difficulty, on Ali Fuad Pasha, the commander of another and much weaker army corps stationed further west, in Ankara. This was a remarkable achievement, since he soon broke with the Sultan's government to become first a simple civilian and then, officially, a civilian rebel.

After his arrival in Anatolia Mustafa Kemal displayed the gift which lay at the root of most of his successes – his ability to work with whatever material was at hand. What was at hand, militarily, were the forces under the two generals, Kâzım Karabekir and Ali Fuad. He made them commanders of the eastern and western front respectively. In addition, there were the popular resistance units, formed spontaneously (by patriots, adventurers, even brigands) in the western areas occupied or threatened with occupation by the Greeks. These Mustafa Kemal tried to incorporate in his western front. Politically there were already in existence nuclei of resistance known as Societies for the Defence of [Ottoman] Rights and Anti-annexation Societies. These Mustafa Kemal proceeded to unify in two congresses from which he emerged as Chairman of the Permanent Executive Committee, his first political title. Emotionally, there were two forces at hand – the personal fear felt by Turkish Muslims threatened with foreign occupation, and the spirit and enthusiasm of Islam. Mustafa Kemal tried to mobilize both forces. His war was to be a Holy War, a *jihad*, in defence of the community of the faithful.

Mustafa Kemal was not without resources, but the obstacles in his path were great. The most important was the moral power of the Sultan and of his government (not the spiritual, for the Sultan, although he might call himself Caliph, was no Pope). The second was particular-ism, for, as we have seen, in spite of centralizing and unifying reforms, which had gathered speed under the Young Turks, the corporate structure of the Ottoman Empire had survived, and members of autonomous groups and institutions knew instinctively that their future was bound up with that of the Sultanate.

The law-abiding nature, even the legalism of the Turks presented yet another difficulty. This legalism was a natural feature of a society which for centuries had been governed under the Holy Law of Islam. But although this respect for the law was of religious origin, it extended also to secular legislation. Turkish society was and, to a large extent, still is paternalistic. In such a society the state, as represented by its official servants, has an aura and a prestige that can easily foil unofficial initiatives. Mustafa Kemal and his associates were not rebels either by temperament or by training. They had all been military or civilian functionaries of the Ottoman state. They wanted to capture the state and reform it, but state authority as such they respected. Yet they had to challenge the existing authority of the state, which was inimical to their plans. They had to challenge it without offending the law-abiding habits of their fellow-countrymen. It was a difficult undertaking, but once again the Allies came unwittingly to the rescue. Once again it was the Allies who helped Mustafa Kemal surmount the obstacles in his path.

In October 1919 Mustafa Kemal reached a tenuous agreement with the Sultan's government. The agreement provided for free elections to a new Chamber of Deputies which, against Mustafa Kemal's wishes, was to meet in Istanbul. The elections were held and the Deputies, some of whom had pledged support to Mustafa Kemal but who were outside his range the moment they set foot in the capital, gathered in Istanbul. The tone of this assembly was more national than nationalist, reflecting the spirit of the National Covenant in defence of the territorial integrity of the core of the Ottoman Empire – of Turkey in other words. This Covenant, which had been drawn up in the two resistance congresses held earlier in Anatolia, was promulgated by the Chamber. The Allies took this as a challenge and occupied Istanbul, where earlier they had been content to exercise indirect pressure. Some of the Deputies were arrested, some of the others escaped to Anatolia. The Sultan's person and the Sultan's government were henceforth under constraint – and whatever they did could now be interpreted as the result of that constraint. This was precisely the excuse which Mustafa Kemal needed. Armed with it, he proceeded to establish the legal foundation of his authority. The Chamber, which the Allies had dispersed and which had formally prorogued itself in Istanbul, was reassembled – with a few additions and minus some absent members – in Ankara under the name of Grand National Assembly. Its opening on 23 April 1920 was preceded by an elaborate religious ceremony. Its members swore to pursue no aim other than the liberation from foreign constraint and the consequent independence of the institution of the Caliphate and of the country at large. In a proclamation, where once again the words Turkey and Turk do not occur but which spoke of saving 'religion's last country', they branded as a lie the allegation that they were rebelling against the Sultan.[15]

Nevertheless, this allegation was believed – largely, it is true, by those who preferred the Sultan's rule to that of the new authority in Ankara. A civil war followed: Circassians and Abkhazes who had been settled along the southern shores of the Sea of Marmora and between Ankara and Istanbul, local notables in the town of Yozgat, east of Ankara, and in Konya south of it, challenged the authority of the new National Assembly. The arguments used by both sides were drawn from religion. Mustafa Kemal's opponents appealed to the decree (*fetva*) issued by the Shaykh al-Islam, the Chief Mufti in Istanbul. Drawn up in the customary form of a question and answer, this decree argued that rebels against the authority of the Sultan deserved to be killed as brigands and that it was incumbent on all Muslims to support the Sultan in putting an end to the rebellion. A counter-decree signed by the Muftis of Anatolia replied that Muslims fighting for the rights of the Caliphate and for territory usurped by foreigners, could not be considered as brigands and that resistance against foreign encroachment was a duty incumbent on all Muslims. The civil war was thus fought round the legality of a Muslim resistance that the Sultan had not ordered. The will to resist was paramount. In fact, it was the resistance party among the Circassians, it was, more precisely, a Circassian swash-buckler called Edhem and the mounted irregulars under his command, who won the Civil War for Mustafa Kemal. Then a second internal operation had to be undertaken against the irregulars themselves. The army of the Grand National Assembly suppressed them as an independent force and Mustafa Kemal, now in complete control of unoccupied Anatolia, turned his attention to the Greek invaders.

The Armenians were no problem: the Eastern Front Commander, Kâzım Karabekir, routed the small Armenian army; only forty-six Turkish officers and men were killed and seventy-six were wounded.[16] The defeat of the Greeks took longer, but was no less spectacular when it came. In July 1921 the Greek army broke through the Turkish front and occupied the two towns of Kütahya and Eskişehir. Mustafa Kemal, whom the Assembly named Commander-in-Chief with extra-ordinary powers, ordered a withdrawal deep enough to allow him to regroup his forces. He then met and held the Greek advance on the river Sakarya. The Assembly rewarded him with the title of *ghazi* or victorious warrior for the faith, and the rank of Marshal. Once Anatolia had been organized for resistance, once the Greeks had been held, there could be no doubt of the ultimate issue. It came a year later when Mustafa Kemal neatly surrounded and destroyed the bulk of the Greek army in western Anatolia, at a cost to his forces of 2,500 killed. It was the end not only of the Greek army, but also of all the Greeks of Asia Minor, who had lived and often prospered under Turkish rule, in some cases for eight centuries. It also presaged the end of the Sultanate.

Both these results were achieved because Mustafa Kemal knew how to bide his time and divide his enemies. On the diplomatic front he had successfully isolated the Greeks. The Sultan's government had been unsuccessful in dividing the Allies and was thus obliged to give in to their united demands as set forth in the stillborn Treaty of Sèvres – a treaty which left to the Turks only Istanbul and a corner of Asia Minor. Against this division Mustafa Kemal secured the support of Bolshevik Russia – a support which became effective only after the Turks had achieved their first military successes, for diplomatic manoeuvre had to have a backing of force, which the Sultan lacked. Next he came to an accommodation with the French. The British, who had originally supported the Greeks, tried their hand at compromise. In any case, their non-involvement was all Mustafa Kemal needed and this he achieved. After the final victory over the Greeks, British good offices were in fact useful in securing the peaceful handing over to the Ankara government of Turkey-in-Europe, including Istanbul.

On the home front, which Mustafa Kemal always considered paramount, his tactics were no less impeccable. Through the Grand National Assembly he mobilized all Muslims willing to resist. As long as the war lasted he refused to discuss permanent constitutional arrange-ments. Against supporters of the Istanbul government, he used irregulars, then threw his new army against them. He even organized his own tame Bolshevik Party to stop genuine Bolshevik infiltration. He isolated the Sultan – presenting him first as a prisoner, then as a traitor in the hands of the Allies. Perhaps his most effective weapon was the ambiguous doctrine of national will and national sovereignty. The first concept was founded in fact, since there was a will to resist, at least among those directly threatened by foreigners. Nor was the second doctrine novel to Turkish politics. The Ottoman Empire had been officially a constitutional monarchy since 1876. What is more, the new nation was the old community of the faithful – one word designated both. In Islam alongside the tradition of obedience to authority, there is a parallel tradition, already alluded to, that the community of the faithful is paramount. The Grand National Assembly included conservatives as well as radicals; Mustafa Kemal's formulas could be interpreted to give satisfaction to both.

The conservatives, it is true, were often alarmed, but they were always out-manoeuvred. Until the end of the war, they were not given a pretext for a break with Mustafa Kemal. The liberation of the institution of the Sultanate receded as a war aim, but religious feeling was not flouted. In the message to the nation which announced the destruction of the Greek army, Mustafa Kemal was still careful to please the pious. 'The valour, force and swiftness of the armies of the Turkish Grand National Assembly,' he wrote, 'have become the instruments of divinely granted victory.'[17] But less than two years after this divinely granted victory, most of the official institutions of Islam were swept away. At the end of August 1922, with the Greeks out of Anatolia, Mustafa Kemal could choose the way along which he would lead the country. If he chose a secular republic, if he willed modern Turkey, it was because the whole development of the Turkish educated élite had headed in that direction. Mustafa Kemal saw the way more clearly than his associates or predecessors, but his vision was neither arbitrary nor accidental.

Why, then, did the Ottoman élite choose secularism as an ideal? The simplest explanation is that if people are schooled in the philosophy of French secularism, they will come to adopt French secularism as an ideal. And French-type secularism was certainly the dominant philosophy of the network of secondary and high schools which the sultans had set up to train the civilian and military officers of their state. The prototype of these schools, the Imperial Lycée of Galatasaray in Istanbul, was avowedly secularist. The Pope would not allow Catholics to attend it, and the Muslim Shaykh al-Islam saw the school in the same light and strongly approved of the papal ban.[18] It is true that the Ottoman lycées had their periods of religious instruction and their lessons of Islamic humanities: Arabic grammar and Persian literature. But these traditional disciplines were attenuated and extraneous. The main aim of the schools was to produce 'enlightened' men in contra-distinction to the mass of Muslim 'fanatics'.

Fanaticism was the accusation which the West – the secular West and also, for tactical reasons, the religious West – directed against Islam. Ottoman Muslims could and did counter it in two ways. They could say that Islam was not a fanatical creed, as witness the toleration which Islamic society displayed towards followers of other religions. They could, therefore, argue that they were Muslims but not fanatics. Or they could tacitly accept the accusation and cease being Muslims in order to become 'modern' men. As Western-type education had already alienated the élite from the mass of Muslims, from among whom they had sprung, it is the second attitude which became the more common. The educated, the 'enlightened' were becoming another nation, whose culture and way of life came to differ from those of the rest of the people. However, right up to the end of the Ottoman Empire and right up to Mustafa Kemal's victory over the Greeks, what the educated élite and the mass of Turkish Muslims had in common overshadowed their differences. Essentially what they had in common was a concern for the preservation of the state. And by their common efforts they did preserve the state. But what emerged from the struggle was not an Ottoman Muslim State for which the soldiers fought, but the national Turkish State which most officers had come to desire.

Peace and prosperity, material well-being, 'development' (to use a modern term) were also a common aim, for Islam was not opposed to economic or industrial progress. In the seventeenth century some Muslim divines may have had their doubts about the religious propriety of printing-presses, but these doubts were quickly dispelled. Mechanical inventions as such were not opposed by orthodox Islam, which also had nothing against factories or industrialization generally. The sultans had always sought to profit from Western military technology – from cannons and muskets to submarines and aircraft – and no Mufti opposed them in this. Industry was not confused with heresy. Indeed, one of the earliest Ottoman ambassadors to Paris – a man usually described as a reactionary, because he disliked the West and also because he allied himself with the Janissaries and suffered their fate – specifically suggested the setting up of 'five factories for snuff, paper, crystal, cloth and porcelain' – which was all the industry he had seen in the West.[19] There were no objections on religious grounds to modern agriculture (one of the earliest steam tractors produced in England was exported to Turkey and used near Adana) or to trade. Banking, it is true, presented some difficulty, as Islam, like medieval Christianity, banned the charging of interest, considering it as usury; but canonical objections to it were circumvented in the second half of the nineteenth century. To present the Muslims as Luddites, as hostile to all invention from the loom to the motor car is, therefore, to travesty the facts.

There seems superficially more substance in the charge that Islam stood in the way of material progress, because of the spirit of fatalism which it inculcated, because of its philosophy of contentment with 'one cloak, one morsel of food' – to use a much-quoted cliché. However, reliance on the will of God had not stopped either Puritans in the West or Muslims in the East, in the ages of Islamic expansion, from bettering their lot and adding to the hardware of the societies in which they lived. A belief in the efficacy of prayer does not imply a belief in the futility of personal endeavour. When the Ottoman armies suffered their major reverses in the Balkan War in 1912, the Shaykh al-Islam asked that all Muslim school-children should repeat an Arabic prayer 4,444 times. This spiritual task may have been excessive, but it was not, as Turkish secularists implied, the cause of the Turkish defeat, for which the secularist Young Turks were themselves largely responsible. There was, it is true, a lack of personal initiative among Ottoman Muslims during the period of decline but its causes had little to do with religion. Bad leadership, the weight of an arbitrary and inefficient bureaucracy, the feeling of despair engendered by successive defeats, and above all the traditional corporate structure of Ottoman society, did induce a feeling

49

of helplessness in individuals. Religion, it is true, consoled them, but it also often stirred them to resistance, as Mustafa Kemal and his comrades-in-arms realized when they appealed to religious sentiment to rouse and lead the Turks of Anatolia against the infidel invader. That war was won by a coalition of national forces, modernist, secularist, conservative, traditionalist. But with victory came a parting of the ways.

The leaders, and above all the one uncontested leader of Turkish resistance, Mustafa Kemal, blamed religion for the backwardness, the material degradation of Anatolian Turks. It was a neat reversal of traditional attitudes. The old traditional leaders in the past and the mass of people in the present believed that impiety caused material ills. The new leaders blamed piety. At first they excepted the principles of pure, pristine Islam from their indictment. It was not Islam as such, but later accretions and superstitions propagated by men exploiting religion for material gain that were responsible, they said. The boundary between superstition and religion was difficult to draw, and after some half-hearted attempts at reforming Islam, the reformers found refuge in confining religion to places of worship, or, more poetically and more restrictively, to the hearts of the faithful. Statecraft was to be guided by secular needs and secular laws alone. But by denying the state any religious aura, they also made it impossible for the mass of believers to feel any personal commitment to it or to its policies.

4   The Republic of Atatürk

TURKEY HAS HAD MANY REFORMERS. Among them Mustafa
Kemal stands out as the most radical and the most consistent. The
development of the modern, secular character of the Turkish state runs
parallel with the development of his personal ascendancy. In September
1922 Mustafa Kemal was the victorious Commander-in-Chief, the
President of the National Assembly and, as such, the head of the
provisional executive, but his power was not absolute. Having assured
himself of military victory and with the unrivalled prestige which that
victory conferred on him he proceeded to eliminate his opponents and
rivals one by one.

Once again the Allies gave him his first opening. They invited both
the Ankara government and the Sultan's government to send repre-
sentatives to the Peace Conference in Lausanne. The Assembly in
Ankara was furious. Mustafa Kemal widened the scope of their anger
from the person of the Sultan Vahdettin and of his Ministers, to the
institution of the Sultanate itself. The modernists among the deputies
wanted nothing better; the conservatives were silenced by a sterner
argument. The sultans had won power by the use of force, Mustafa
Kemal argued. In the course of the Turkish War of Independence it had
been wrenched from them by force. If their supporters refused to
recognize that accomplished fact they stood in danger of losing their
heads. The conservatives preferred to keep their heads, and the law
abolishing the Sultanate was passed by the Assembly on 1 November
1922. On 17 November Vahdettin fled from Istanbul on board the
British battleship *Malaya*. An interregnum followed. Mustafa Kemal

remained President of the Assembly. But in Istanbul there was a potential focus of alternative allegiance. While suppressing the Sultanate, the Assembly had preserved the institution of Caliphate, conceived unhistorically, as one of spiritual leadership over Muslims throughout the world.

An elderly Ottoman prince, Abdul Mejid, was appointed Caliph by the sovereign Assembly. He was to prove a weak opponent, but before he could be dealt with, the opposition within the Assembly in Ankara had to be disarmed. In December 1922 they made an unsuccessful attempt to prevent Mustafa Kemal from standing again as Deputy. Mustafa Kemal organized his supporters in a solid front under the name of People's Party. The party, he said, would be national and comprehensive. It would also be 'a school for the political education' of the Turkish people. It was a novel concept, for the old Ottoman Constitution had envisaged free elections without the benefit of political education. The People's Party was formed on 9 September 1923 and duly elected Mustafa Kemal to lead it. It also duly won the elections to the second Assembly which, on 11 August 1923, again chose Mustafa Kemal to be its President.

In the meantime Turkey had made peace with the Allies. The Treaty of Lausanne, signed on 24 July 1923, ratified the Turkish victory. The independence of Turkey was recognized, foreign extraterritorial rights and privileges, known as 'capitulations', were ended, the remaining allied armies of occupation withdrawn. All the Greeks in Turkey, apart from the reduced community in Istanbul, were expelled in exchange for the smaller number of Turks in Greece, outside western Thrace. As there were practically no Armenians left in the country, again outside Istanbul, Turkish children could now recite a poem starting with the lines 'Anatolia, Anatolia – full of Turks from end to end!' It was not a completely accurate description, since there were in Anatolia Muslims who were not Turks, but the distinction between the two concepts was novel and vague.

On 29 October 1923, after an artifically engineered cabinet crisis (which was meant to prove and did prove that the opposition was powerless to form an alternative government), the Assembly proclaimed a Republic and elected Mustafa Kemal to be its first President. The interregnum was over, but the conservative, gradualist or liberal opposition was not yet disarmed. Although Mustafa Kemal was elected President by the unanimous vote of 158 deputies, there were more than one hundred abstentions. What is more, the opposition was joined by the three leading nationalist generals who had worked with Mustafa Kemal in organizing resistance in Anatolia. However, Mustafa Kemal was not to be stopped in his course. A few months later, in March 1924, he pushed through the Assembly his most radical reform – the abolition of the Caliphate, the expulsion from Turkey of all the members of the Ottoman dynasty, the closure of religious schools, and the abolition of the Ministry of the Holy Law (*sharia*) and of Pious Foundations. These measures, which are usually described as the disestablishment of Islam in Turkey, were once again justified in religious terms. The object, Mustafa Kemal explained, was to disentangle religion from politics and, by so doing, to liberate, elevate, even to revive it. Ottoman reforms, it will be remembered, had always been recommended to the public on the grounds that they fulfilled the precepts of the Holy Law of Islam. Now the institutions of Islam were being suppressed in the name of the higher interests of that religion. It was the last time the excuse was to be used. The appeal would henceforth be to the values of 'civilization'. But before civilization could be established, the opposition had to be suppressed. In November 1924, Mustafa Kemal's opponents, led by a former comrade-in-arms Rauf Orbay and by a group of other former members of the People's Party, formed an opposition Progressive Party. Their appeal was to 'democracy' – an appeal that had been heard before (when freedom and the constitution had been the watchwords of malcontents) and which was to be repeated several times in the history of the Turkish Republic.

The Progressive Party had a short life. In February 1925 a revolt broke out among the Kurds in eastern Turkey. Although this revolt had overtones of Kurdish nationalism, it was, in the main, of conservative and religious inspiration. Its leader, Said, was a *shaykh* of the Nakshibendi order of dervishes, an order that was intertwined with the organization of many Kurdish tribes. Its flag was the green flag of Islam. The revolt was suppressed and with it the opposition in Turkey. The Progressive Party dissolved itself, while protesting its innocence of any complicity in the revolt. Individual opponents of the regime found themselves before Independence Tribunals – organs of political repression that had been first instituted during the war against the Greeks in Anatolia. There were many executions – of rebel Kurds as well as of Turkish enemies of the regime – and more deportations. Some opposition politicians were sent to prison or into exile. Two years of political repression followed, at the end of which there was not only no opposition left, but also hardly anyone capable of forming one, while Mustafa Kemal became the undisputed sole ruler of Turkey. It was also during this period that the secularization of the country was completed.

The Nakshibendi revolt in eastern Turkey was followed in September 1925 by the suppression of all dervish orders and the closure of Muslim shrines. 'The truest order,' Mustafa Kemal declared, 'is the order of civilization.' He added, 'We draw our strength from civilization, scholarship and science. We do not accept anything else.'[20] This was not only a secularist, but a positivist manifesto. Simultaneously with the suppression of the dervishes, the Assembly banned the wearing of the fez (*tarboosh*) and turbans – forms of headgear with distinctively Islamic associations.

Religious courts had already been closed down – in April 1924, soon after the abolition of the Caliphate. Now a final break was made with the Holy Law of Islam. In February 1926 the Assembly adopted the Swiss Civil Code. The Holy Law had already been whittled down in Ottoman times until it regulated little more than the personal status of Muslims. It was now driven out of this last reserve: marriage, divorce, inheritance were to be arranged as in Western Europe. Polygamy, divorce at the husband's behest, inequality of women's shares in the division of estates were abolished. A new commercial code, based on the Italian model, a new penal code and a new law of contract were also enacted. The whole edifice was completed in April 1928 when the Assembly deleted from the Constitution the reference to Islam as the official religion of the state. Repression had done its work. All 269 Deputies present voted unanimously for this final measure of secularization. Then in November 1928, use of the Arabic alphabet was banned and an adapted form of the Latin alphabet was introduced as the official Turkish alphabet.

Most of these measures were carried out in an atmosphere of repression. After the suppression of the Kurdish revolt, the discovery of a plot against Mustafa Kemal's life led to the liquidation of his opponents among the élite. The opposition generals were acquitted of complicity in the plot, but they were nevertheless banished from politics. Surviving Young Turk leaders were less lucky – some of them were hanged, others exiled. This part of the repression resulted in the unification of the governing élite.

With no prominent rivals left, there was no danger of coups or juntas. Mustafa Kemal had been a successful general and it was military victory in the field that had won him power. His Prime Minister, Ismet Pasha (who later took the surname Inönü, from the name of the village where he twice defeated the Greeks) had been his Chief of Staff and Front Commander. Some of his ministers, many of his leading officers had also come from the Army. But the Army as such was kept out of politics and government. Mustafa Kemal handed it over to a strict disciplinarian, Marshal Fevzi Çakmak, an old Ottoman General who had been slow in joining the nationalists in Ankara, but who gave them faithful service once he had made up his mind. Under Çakmak the Army, or rather the officer corps, was a disciplined and on the whole contented pillar of the state. But the Army was kept under close supervision. Retired generals were sure of good jobs in the Party or the state bureaucracy, but they had to retire first. It was not only repression that had united the governing élite around the person of Mustafa Kemal. His enemies were, to a large extent, their enemies. The dervish *shaykhs* of Anatolia, political adventurers of the Young Turkish type, ambitious generals – all threatened the solidarity of an established and widespread bureaucracy – civil and military, present and future. The future bureaucrats were the students, for the majority of those studying at the University of Istanbul and at the new university in Ankara which Mustafa Kemal established in 1925, as well as all the students at military academies, were preparing themselves for service to the state. The division of the Turks into two camps – 'western' and 'eastern', 'progressive' and 'reactionary', 'civilized' and 'ignorant' was hardening. This division went back to the early Ottoman reforms, but it had been obscured by common allegiance to Islam, an allegiance that was genuine in the case of the people, and often nominal in that of the élite. But with secularism, this common bond was snapped. Although Mustafa Kemal remained a focus of unity, the two camps saw him in different lights. To the people he was the *ghazi*, the man who defeated the infidels; to the élite he was the champion of progress. He was also champion of the supremacy of the interests of the 'civilized' class – a class which grew under his rule, as Western-type education spread, but which remained a minority in the country. The 'civilized' were a cultural and social class – but they were not a caste, just as the old Ottoman Civil Service had not been quite a closed caste. Education secured admission to it. To join the ruling class, the Easterner had to be westernized, the ignorant to be civilized. And many did just that. When the Republic was formed, the proportion of literate Turks – literate, of course, in the old Arabic alphabet and educated both in Eastern and Western disciplines, stood at roughly ten per cent. This number grew gradually until today it represents over forty per cent of the population – all of whom have been schooled in 'Western culture'.

The philosophy which Mustafa Kemal inculcated in the ruling class is generally described as 'populism' which should be defined as service to the people, rather than government by the people. 'The peasant is our master', Mustafa Kemal said even before the Greeks were driven out of Anatolia, but the ruling élite decided where the interests of the master lay. The rule of Mustafa Kemal, 'Father of the Turks', was paternalistic. The bureaucracy inherited the traditions of Ottoman paternalism. The single party – the Republican People's Party – was, as we have seen, a school for the people and not an alternative channel through which the people's wishes and grievances could be expressed. Secularism blocked the traditional parallel channel of communication, that of the religious institution, or rather institutions. In Ottoman times there had originally been two branches of government, the religious and the military, the religious subsuming the civil branch. The reforms had made the civil branch autonomous, but, although much reduced in status, the religious hierarchy of Muftis with the Shaykh al-Islam at its head, had retained at least a nominal importance until the Republic. In Anatolia the dervish orders were more real, autonomous centres of power. The religious institution had been as democratic in its methods of recruitment as the state Civil Service, since scholarship in Muslim learning, acquired in *medreses*, was the passport to the highest religious offices. However, although nominally distinct, the official hierarchy of the *ulema*, of canon law scholars, was usually in alliance with and sub-servient to the state. The dervish brotherhoods had more freedom. They were also closer to the people. They were foci of popular piety, centres of social cohesion. They provided the countryside with its saints and its advisers. When the Republic banned them, some disappeared, others survived clandestinely. As for the Muftis, they became minor state functionaries, ill-paid and generally ignored. In these conditions, the bureaucracy, to which the Republican People's Party quickly assimilated itself, was supreme. To the people it presented a united front: the village schoolteacher, the tax-gatherer, the gendarme, the district officer, all represented the state. And the state had an immense job to do.

The country was largely devastated. With the departure of the indigenous Greeks and Armenians and of many foreigners, there was an immense, in some cases almost total shortage of skills. The million or so refugees who came in – largely from the Balkans – were mostly peasants who could not take the place of Greek and Armenian crafts-men. The settlement of these refugees was the first major test for the Republican bureaucracy. According to the short-lived Opposition Progressive Party, the job was bungled. To calculate the compensation payable for property which the refugees left behind in their countries of origin, to apportion among them property abandoned in Turkey by Greeks and Armenians, to resettle the indigent – these were tasks that any civil service would have found difficult. It is no wonder that the Turkish Civil Service fell down on the job, that abuses were rampant, that many members of the ruling party became rich overnight in contrast with the surrounding destitution. The brave decision to build a new capital in Ankara in the centre of the country made additional demands on the Civil Service as well as on economic resources. It also affected unfavourably the administration of the main commercial centre in Istanbul. And as reforms and innovations followed each other, the state took on more and more work. The unification of the school systems, in other words the closing down of religious schools, and the subsequent expansion of higher education, led to a massive increase of state activity in the educational field.

Mustafa Kemal's original economic policy was to encourage indigenous Turkish private enterprise within a mixed and largely state-regulated economy. But the main economic enterprises in the country had been foreign-owned, and these were nationalized one by one. The railways, the country's sole important coalfield at Zonguldak on the Black Sea, harbours and utilities all came to be run by the state. This policy was accentuated after the world economic crisis of 1929, when state capitalism (*étatisme*) became official dogma. Before 1929, a buoyant world commodity market had kept the country's weak economy afloat. Even so, Turkey's exports declined steadily from 1925 onwards, a trend which was not reversed until the middle of the Second World War, when Germany and the Allies tried to deny each other Turkish produce by the wholesale use of the so-called policy of pre-emptive buying. The 1929 crisis deprived Turkey of foreign trade credits. Until then Turkey could run a trading deficit; after the crisis there had to be more exports than imports. With declining exports, this meant that imports had to be slashed to a level which was inadequate to cover consumption, let alone investment. Between 1929 and 1931 Turkey's imports were halved and the 1929 figure was not reached again until after the Second World War.[21]

In the inter-war years the major economic effort of the Republican government was directed at extending the railway network. This obsession with railways (which today in Turkey lose money as regularly as they do elsewhere), derived from the war-time experiences of Mustafa Kemal and of his associates whose military campaigns had been hampered by lack of communications, as well as from a vision of an industrial society dating back to the railway age. On the other hand roads were neglected. So, too, was agriculture, the mainstay of the country's economy. Agricultural productivity did not rise; even the area under cultivation did not increase substantially until after the Second World War. Industrialization, by which the Republican government set so much store, was also a slow starter, and it was not until the 1930s that Turkey's first modern factories were built – a group of textile factories established with Soviet aid. Just before the Second

World War, Turkey's first steel mill was built with British aid. These factories, and a few sugar refineries, more or less exhaust the extent of Turkish industrialization in the first years of the Republic, and they all belonged to the state. Large-scale private initiative was at that time conspicuously absent.

However, if the economic achievements of the Republic were for a long time meagre, the government was not wholly to blame. Lack of skills and capital, a legacy of under-development, war devastation, and the world economic crisis, were largely responsible. It remains never-theless true that while the institutions of the country were given a modern look, the economy from which they drew their strength remained backward and the society round them desperately poor. The Republic did not witness an economic miracle; nor did it mobilize the creative energies of the Turkish people. Whether these energies could have been mobilized by other means and a miracle achieved, is, of course, another question. But the lack of development outside Ankara, outside the few factories and railway extensions which we have mentioned, and the small new middle-class suburbs of Istanbul and Izmir, is a fact – a fact which explains the subsequent course of Turkish politics. The Turkish novelist Orhan Kemal's description of an exile's return to his home town, was generally true of provincial Turkey during the inter-war years. 'My home town,' he wrote on his return to Adana, 'suddenly seemed in ruins. Joyless streets, lean cats, rows of padlocked shops, abandoned by bankrupt owners. . . . Roads stretching point-lessly under the hot sun, wooden houses losing their plaster.'[22]

It is not surprising that state capitalism attracted criticism. The second free opposition party permitted by Mustafa Kemal, the Free Republican Party, in the few months of its existence in 1930, fought specifically for economic liberalism. After its dissolution, the ruling Republican People's Party co-opted a few workers and peasants into its single list of candidates (who were of course automatically elected), but otherwise intensified bureaucratic control over the country.

Ankara was the administrative and intellectual centre of the Republican bureaucracy and Ankara was all that Orhan Kemal's Adana was not. It was the seat of Parliament, controlled, it is true, by a single party but potentially capable of serving democratic purposes, of an impressive array of ministries, of a new university, of state banks and state industrial boards. It was also the centre of the new secular Western society which Mustafa Kemal sought to create by his reforms. Just as the political order of the Turkish Republic had been modelled on that of France, or rather of an ideal secular France, so Turkish society was conceived in French terms. It was a nineteenth-century French wellwisher who, on being asked where the salvation of Turkey lay, replied, 'Ouvrez les femmes, fermez le Coran.' This precept was followed to the letter. The veiling of women was officially discouraged; the introduction of the Swiss Civil Code gave them civil equality with men, and nominal political equality followed. In 1930 women were admitted to municipal elections, in 1934 to Parliament. Hand-picked women were encouraged to demonstrate their equality by obtaining appointments in the Civil Service, the judiciary, schools and universities, politics, the professions. Not only social life, but also society life was to be as in Western Europe: balls and dances, beauty contests, the radio, competitive sports were all officially introduced. Sunday replaced Friday as the official day of rest.

Finally, in 1935, all Turks were told to choose European-type surnames, and Turkish translations for 'Mr' and 'Mrs' were invented. The reform of the Turkish language, the substitution of 'pure' Turkish words for terms drawn from Arabic and Persian, languages that stood to Turkish roughly as Latin and Greek stand to English – was pushed forward vigorously. As was the case with other innovations, the language reform movement could trace its beginnings to late Ottoman times, when it was propagated by a few nationalist intellectuals. Under Mustafa Kemal it became official policy to such an extent that official 'pure' Turkish threatened to become an unintelligible form of Mandarin, just as 'high Ottoman' had been under the sultans. The movement was then restrained in accordance with a newly invented 'Sun Theory of Language'. This propounded that as all languages were derived from Turkish, foreign words could be used in Turkish, since they had originally been Turkish words. Nevertheless many of the neologisms stuck, including some that were transparent imitations of European forms – *okul* for school, from the French *école*; *genel* for 'general'; *onur* for 'honour', or the adjectival ending -sel from the

French -el (-elle). A new science of history was constructed on similar lines: it purported to prove not so much that the Turks were European, but that all Europeans had been Turks.

With all its exaggerations and its occasional absurdities, the new Turkish *persona* had some foundation in fact. Even before the Republic, an Ottoman liberal or a Young Turkish officer finding himself in Western Europe felt a European and looked a European the moment he discarded the fez. He had already been schooled in European culture, he delighted in European entertainment, he was at least as secular as his European counterpart. The same was true of the Ottoman élite in Istanbul – including society ladies with their English nannies and French novels. Mustafa Kemal simply applied ideally to the whole country (and actually to the Republican ruling class) what westernized Ottomans had already practised or hoped to practise. The new Turkish *persona* was thus a mixture of fact and wishful thinking – the proportion of fact increasing as the years went by. For Mustafa Kemal's conception was inspired by the clear realization that 'civilization', as he called it, or technological civilization as we prefer to call it today, is one and un-divided, and that it leads to uniformity of culture in the widest sense of that term. So, to the extent that Turkey has become a technological society, the Turks have become 'Europeans' (or modern men) in their way of life. The limiting factor is, of course, not so much the historically different origin of Turkish culture as the distances which still separates Turkey from the economic and social norms of a modern technological society.

The newness of Mustafa Kemal's new look obscured that distance. Official propaganda tended to present the Republic as a progressive, developing, almost a developed country. Descriptions of backwardness in the past were encouraged; backwardness in the present was not a proper subject for discussion in polite society. There were of course good reasons for this attitude. Mustafa Kemal had set himself the task of inspiring self-confidence among his fellow-countrymen. His much-quoted slogans, 'Turk! Work, be proud, be confident!' or 'Happy is the man who calls himself a Turk', his public insistence that the Turks were a hard-working, an intelligent nation (coupled with private doubts about the ability of many of his subordinates) were meant to inspire, and, to some extent, did inspire solid achievement.

61

In the late 'thirties there was a gradual improvement in the country's economic fortunes. This is often attributed to the first five-year plan of industrialization, buttressed with subsidies and tariff protection. Perhaps a more important factor was the slow revival of world trade (and the greater availability of credits) just before the Second World War. But the first modest advances whetted the appetite for real prosperity, and, as usual, the omnipotent state received more blame than praise. State capitalism once again came under fire and in 1937 Mustafa Kemal, by now a sick man, met criticism by changing his Prime Minister.

After presiding for fourteen years over the executive machinery of state, Ismet Inönü saw himself replaced by a man thought to be more liberal in his economic outlook – Celâl Bayar, who had until then run the main state-supported commercial bank. However, arguments about the economy were not the only reasons for the change. Even more important was Mustafa Kemal's determination to press for the return to Turkey of the province of Alexandretta (Iskenderun). This province, for which republican Turkey chose the 'pure' Turkish name of Hatay (Cathay), had been lost to French-mandated Syria after the First World War. However, in recognition of the large numbers of Turks who inhabited it, it was given a measure of administrative autonomy. Now with the home front quiet, and, more significantly, with the Great Powers courting Turkey's friendship, as a new world war grew daily nearer, Mustafa Kemal saw his chance to pull more Turks into his national state. Where Ismet Inönü had counselled caution, Mustafa Kemal went on boldly to press France into a bargain highly advantageous to Turkey.[23] In exchange for a treaty of friendship with France, Turkish troops were allowed into the disputed province. A year later Hatay became Turkish. Ironically, when this extension of Turkish territory was achieved, Inönü was President of the Republic. Mustafa Kemal died a few months earlier, on 10 November 1938.

The annexation of Hatay, which gave Turkey what it had lacked before – a serviceable harbour along its southern shore – was a fitting close to Mustafa Kemal's efforts to build a national Turkish State. He had won for it all the territory he could. He had also the courage to write off what was irredeemable – the Turks in the Balkans, the scattered

Turkish communities in the Arab world, and, most important, the tempting, but dangerous dream of a Great Turan in Asia. Already in 1923, Turkey was in the post-Versailles classification a 'have' country and, as such, it tended naturally to the side of the Western democracies against those that deemed themselves 'have-nots' – Nazi Germany, Fascist Italy and Stalinist Russia. The foreign policy of the Turkish Republic, about which much has been written, was in fact a fairly consistent reflection of its territorial contentment. Its main need was consolidation and conservation, hence Mustafa Kemal's foreign policy slogan, 'Peace at home and peace abroad.'

Consolidation required, or at least did not preclude, some adjustments. The annexation of Hatay was one. The Convention of Montreux, concluded in 1936, was another. Under it, Turkey regained control over the Straits, which it was allowed to remilitarize. Britain and France, which, after the First World War, had wished to see the Straits demilitarized, were only too happy to have them again defended by the Turks, this time against the ambitions of Mussolini. Earlier, one adjustment could not be effected. At Lausanne Turkey had claimed the province of Mosul, which had been occupied by British troops at the end of the First World War. The province did have quite a large number of Turks living in it, but the majority of its population consisted of Kurds and Muslim and Christian Arabs, who, as a League of Nations commission found, preferred union with Iraq to union with Turkey. Britain took a stand on the Commission's report, and Mustafa Kemal, accepting the fact that he had no means to overcome British opposition, formally abandoned his claim in 1926. The claim was never revived, and Turkish foreign policy from 1926 to the outbreak of the Second World War normally coincided with that of the Western democracies. In the late 'thirties, when war began to threaten, Turkey took part in two regional groupings, both, as it proved, ineffective. In the West, it joined a Balkan Entente, which Hitler, working through Bulgaria, had no difficulty in undermining. In the East, Turkey, Persia, Iraq and Afghanistan concluded the Saadabad Pact, which was equally meaningless. Both groupings aimed at preserving the *status quo*, an aim which Turkey was almost alone in achieving, by a combination of prudence and good luck. Prudence was also the motive force of Mustafa Kemal's policy towards Russia. In the Turkish War of Independence he obtained such support as he could from the Soviets, while resisting both Communist infiltration and the territorial claims advanced by Moscow on behalf of Georgia and Armenia. But after he had made his peace with the West at Lausanne, he kept the Russians at arm's length. However, after the 1929 economic crisis, when Western credits became unobtainable, he accepted Soviet help in building textile factories. Turkish Communists he continued to keep under strict surveillance – in and out of prison – as long as he lived.

These measures against the Communists derived naturally from a policy that was much less radical than was supposed at the time, a policy which was applied by a government ruling over a surprisingly static society. True, there was growth: a slow growth of industry, a growth of railway communications, a real, but comparatively slow growth of literacy, and a growth of population – from 13,600,000 in 1927 to 16,200,000 in 1940. But the pressures of growth were comparatively light: the population had not outstripped land resources and the country could still feed itself; the process of urbanization was slow, as the peasants had not yet started to migrate to the cities in any considerable numbers; a fairly limited educational establishment could still cope with effective demand; above all, a conservative financial policy successfully avoided inflation, while limiting economic growth. Although the seeds of growth, of dynamism and, consequently, of social conflict, were being sown, such a society could still be managed from above. It was the reign of the President, the Prime Minister, ministers, provincial governors and district commissioners, *gendarmerie* commanders, civil servants and teachers. People knew their places. Intrigues, hurried visits to Ankara to outflank a local official were, of course, possible, but the system as such was unchallenged. If it restricted initiative, it also made for stability. It could, and did on occasion, give rise to bureaucratic injustice, but injustice could be tempered by traditional social forces – through the help of friends or relatives, by direct appeal to the rulers, who were by-and-large well-intentioned and in whose waiting-rooms one could always wait until one obtained redress.

Seen from outside, the state of the country looked a distinct improvement on what had prevailed before. There was an impression of progress that was not completely unjustified, however much it was exaggerated. There was a Turkish presence in the world – the 'sick man' had been cured. Playing off one Turk against another was no longer a game that foreigners could easily indulge in; Mustafa Kemal seemed to have unified the country. He had, in fact, unified the educated ruling class, which identified itself with the Republic and accepted the goal of a secular, progressive, industrial, 'Western' society. The danger lay in the possibility of forgetting that the educated ruling class was small, that the new middle-class suburbs of Istanbul, Ankara and Izmir were not representative of the country; the danger lay, in brief, in confusing partly realized aspirations with reality. In 1935, three years before Mustafa Kemal died, eighty-four per cent of all Turks were still illiterate and thus outside the reach of the progressive Republic. Still, the number of those actively hostile to the Republic was small; the number of people actively hostile to Mustafa Kemal Atatürk even smaller. After all, he had dispelled the alien, infidel threat which had hung over the very existence of the Muslim Turkish people. And so when Atatürk died on 10 November 1938, grief was genuinely universal. He had, as he had himself said, reversed the ill-luck that had for centuries dogged the steps of the Turks.

5 Turkey after Atatürk

CHANGE AFTER ATATÜRK WAS SLOW and the outbreak of the Second World War made it even slower. Ismet Inönü, who had been Atatürk's Prime Minister during the formative years of the Republic, became the new President. He pardoned and reintegrated into the regime some of Atatürk's opponents, who had by then grown old and harmless, but otherwise continued the same policies, except that he was by nature a careful man who not only looked before he leapt, but preferred not to leap at all. However, the static society of the middle years of the Republic began to change. Factions appeared in the governing class of the educated Turks. It may be convenient to classify them as left, right and liberal, if one remembers that the first two were equally authoritarian, while the liberals came from the small but growing commercial middle class and were thus anti-authoritarian, as were the remaining conservatives and the majority of the people. But free enterprise had as little chance as the free expression of dissent in the one year before and the five years of the Second World War. In the universities and the press the Left and the Right fought it out. The Left inveighed against the poverty and backwardness of the country, particularly of the villages, and sought to promote remedial state action. The Right was nationalist, if not racialist, and saw the state as an army, a horde on the move in which individuals merged. Authoritarian ideas were reflected in official nomenclature. Inönü was the 'National Leader', to distinguish him from Atatürk, who was posthumously awarded the title 'Eternal Leader'. On national holidays the main thoroughfares were decorated with streamers inscribed with the slogan 'One nation, one party, one leader'. Except in one instance, this was a surface silliness, for a pre-technological society, permeated with economic and social pressure groups, cannot easily support a totalitarian structure. The one exception was a confiscatory capital levy imposed on non-Muslims in the middle years of the war. The idea that non-Muslim merchants, businessmen and artisans prospered while Muslims suffered privation, came easily to the Turks, removed, as they were, by only a generation from the closing century of the Ottoman Empire, a century which was indeed one of Muslim impoverishment and humiliation and of Christian renascence. In a way the capital levy was a revival of the practice of soaking the Christian and Jewish moneylenders of Galata (the business quarter of Istanbul), a practice to which the sultans resorted in times of stringency. There was this difference: the non-Muslim communities now numbered not several millions, but a bare 300,000, and their economic importance, although out of proportion to their numbers, was by no means absolute. Secondly, the levy discriminated not only between Muslims and non-Muslims, but also between the majority of Muslims and a small minority descended from Jews who had been converted to Islam, in some cases three centuries earlier. This type of discrimination, which was wholly alien to the traditions of Muslim Turkish society, had clearly been inspired by Nazi racialism. It was fortunately short-lived.

However, left-wing ideas were, if anything, more successful than Nazi-inspired ideas among the governing class, or, more precisely, the sons of the rulers, and it was in education that they had their widest application. While the immense achievements of the Republic continued to be extolled in official propaganda, the problems of underdevelopment, and, in particular, of rural backwardness and illiteracy were beginning to make themselves felt. In 1940, after preliminary studies which contrasted favourably with the happy-go-lucky arbitrariness of so much republican legislation, Village Institutes were launched which combined academic and vocational learning. They trained leaders for the villages from the villages. It was the most radical educational measure adopted by the Republic, but it was vitiated by prevailing authoritarian tendencies, by an itch to transform society. The Institutes were aggressively secularist, even anti-religious. The teachers trained in them were imposed on the villages as social engineers, as privileged members of the community enjoying free accommodation and land. Rural converts to progress, they were all the more impatient to break existing social moulds with the tactlessness of converts. They were far from being popular, and soon the cry went up that the Institutes were training a corps of Communist commissars.

A programme of accelerated school-building in the villages was similarly resented. The schools had to be built by the villagers them-selves to official specifications. The education they gave was nationalist and secularist. Religious instruction was banned. Legal compulsion rather than tact and persuasion was used to enrol girls, who had been traditionally excluded from rural education. Village Institutes, village primary schools, girls' institutes in the cities and a network of People's Houses and People's Rooms, run by the Republican People's Party, were all intended to drag the country into the twentieth century, and, in varying degrees, they were all resented.

During the war, the Right was pro-German, the Left pro-Allied and their fortunes fluctuated with the military fortunes of the two camps. But involvement in war was what both Inönü and most of the Turks wanted least. In this respect Turkey was like other small European national states, most of which were dragged into the war against their will. Turkey was luckier – comparatively remote from the epicentre of the conflict; it was also thought a difficult country to conquer and to hold. Finally, unlike Yugoslavia or Rumania it had no pressing ethnic minority problem which could be used by the Germans to prise it open. Freed of the necessity to fight, Inönü could concentrate on resisting outside blandishments to join this or that camp, and also on holding in check local hotheads. It was not an insuperably difficult task, as the Turks had had their fill of wars before the Republic, and were, on the whole, as determined as their President to stay out of this one. So although Turkey had treaties of alliance with Britain and France when the war started, a non-aggression treaty with Germany was soon added. As the tide of war turned against the Nazis, so Turkey's neutrality took on an increasingly pro-Allied hue, until war against Germany was declared as a formality in February 1945. However, it was not Germany that most Turks feared, but Soviet Russia. Already in 1939, the Soviet government had asked for a share in the control of the Straits. Consequently, when in the middle of the war British military equipment was sent to Turkey, partly to give the Turks the means of resisting a German onslaught, partly as an inducement to join the Allies, much of it found its way to the Turkish army standing guard over the frontier with Russia. As soon as the war ended, the Russian threat assumed a concrete shape. At the Potsdam Conference, Stalin demanded a revision of the Montreux Convention governing the use of the Turkish Straits. Britain and America agreed with the Soviet demand that the Straits should always be open to the warships of the Black Sea powers and, in principle, remain closed to those of outside powers. Turkey too was willing to consider such a provision. But a further Soviet demand that the Soviet Union should be allowed to join in the defence of the Straits was rejected by Turkey, with the backing of the West. However, Soviet claims were not limited to demands for the control of the Straits. In March 1945 the Soviet government refused to extend the Turkish-Soviet Non-Aggression Treaty, which had originally been concluded in 1925. When the Turkish government enquired through its ambassador in Moscow on what conditions a new agreement could be concluded, it was informed by the Soviet Foreign Minister, Mr Molotov, that in addition to bases in the Straits, Russia claimed a part of eastern Turkey. The claim was assumed to refer to the districts of Kars, Artvin and Ardahan, which Czarist Russia (and then the short-lived Armenian and Georgian Republics) had held between 1878 and 1921. In addition, the Moscow press advanced an unofficial claim on behalf of Soviet Georgia for the eastern half of Turkey's Black Sea coast. It was a revival, in a new guise, of the old threat to detach from Turkey the 'Pontus area', an area which before the First World War had many Greek and Armenian inhabitants, but which had by now become almost entirely Turkish.

That these claims were unwelcome to the West was perfectly clear to Inönü's government, but effective Western support could not be taken for granted until March 1947 when, with the proclamation of the Truman Doctrine, the United States underwrote the existing frontiers of Turkey (and Greece) as well as the continued existence of non-Communist governments in the two countries.

What kind of non-Communist government Turkey was to have was not, however, clear. The war had slowed down the country's development. Half a million men had been kept under arms. As a result, the birth-rate fell from nine per cent for the five years between 1935 and 1940, to six per cent for the subsequent five years. Imports were in short supply and were regularly exceeded by exports. Industrialization slowed down. Shortages and economic mismanagement pushed up the cost of living to over three times its pre-war level. War-time controls worked badly: there was some rationing, but a more extensive black market; the issue of foreign trade permits was inefficient and corrupt; supplies were requisitioned and then allowed to rot for want of proper storage; labour conscription was introduced in mining and was applied so harshly that it was remembered with resentment a generation later. The failure was administrative rather than political, the Civil Service having once again been charged with a task well beyond its capacity. Inönü's administration was generally held responsible. The governing Republican People's Party and its leaders were conceded one achievement: they had kept Turkey out of the war. But at home they had used compulsion and denied freedom, while failing to achieve a tolerable level of competence in the management of the country's affairs. The pressure of discontent was reinforced by the pressure of change. Slow as change had been during the war, the static, paternalistic society of Atatürk's later years was gradually being eroded.

Change was, however, largely confined to the cities, whose growth was beginning to exceed that of the country's population as a whole. Young intellectuals – whether right-wing, left-wing or liberal – were beginning to show less respect for the official guardians. Contractors, war-time speculators, middlemen of all kinds, as well as Turkish merchants who had benefited from the discrimination to which non-Muslims were subject, came to swell the class of entrepreneurs. This class was largely parasitical on the state, but was nevertheless impatient of official restraint and critical of official incompetence. In the countryside too, long years of service in the army had shaken a static structure and brought more knowledge of the outside world at a time when that world, in the shape of urban administrators, was being particularly oppressive. Requisitioning, forced labour, higher taxes, shortages of manufactured goods – all these were not new to Anatolian peasants, who had seen much harsher treatment in the past, but this did not make

70

them more palatable. To make matters worse, secularization had been accentuated, particularly in education. So discontent was fed from many sources. Even the small band of local fascists were discontented, who found themselves in gaol at the end of the war. Discontent had a common target: the bureaucracy and its political arm, the Republican People's Party. Against this it advanced a common demand for more freedom. Freedom was demanded by conservative and progressive, merchant and worker, city dweller and peasant, communist, fascist and liberal. More internal freedom was sure to please the Western Allies, whose help was so necessary against Soviet Russia's threat. But, as in the case of the reforms introduced by the Ottoman sultans in the nine-teenth century, it would be wrong to attribute liberalization solely to external agencies. Outside forces and pressures may have tilted the balance, but there was enough internal pressure to lift the scales of change.

Ismet Inönü's personality was certainly itself an extremely important factor. He was not so much a dictator, as an expert manipulator of internal forces. At the end of the war, he chose at first a policy of cautious liberalization. The formation of opposition parties was allowed, and one of them, the Democratic Party, organized by deputies who had resigned from the Republican People's Party, immediately became the focus of all discontented forces. Founded by Celâl Bayar, Atatürk's last Prime Minister, and other ex-Republicans, amongst whom Adnan Menderes was pre-eminent by the force of his attractive, if unstable, personality, the Democratic Party emerged as a serious rival to the Republicans only a few months after its formation. The threat came as a surprise to Inönü, and his first reaction was to re-impose pressure. Elections were brought forward and held in conditions of administrative interference. Despite this, the Democrats succeeded in returning sixty-four members to the Assembly. How many seats they would have won if the elections had been fairly conducted it is impossible to say, but subsequent events suggest that they may well have won the majority of seats. After the elections, press censorship was tightened and the opposition subjected to administrative harassment. At the same time, Inönü tried to please his right-wing critics by jettisoning his left-wing supporters. Minor repression only exacerbated the situation and in 1947, the year of the Truman Doctrine, Inönü decided that the country could no longer be run by a paternalistic single party. An authoritarian Prime Minister was replaced by a more liberal one, and the Democratic Party opposition was allowed to function normally. Inönü's conversion to democracy was genuine and final. He had been in charge of a paternalistic single-party state under Atatürk and then during his own regime. Now he saw that it was no longer possible or even desirable to run the country from above. He hoped that the Republican People's Party had made enough converts to keep it in power, or at least return it to power after an interval, during which the forces of discontent would be discredited as an alternative government. Inönü's hope was disappointed. In May 1950, in elections that were undeniably free from any kind of pressure (probably for the first time in Turkish history), the Democratic Party won 396 seats out of 487 in the National Assembly. It is true that the mechanics of the electoral law distorted the popular vote. The Democrats' share of the poll was in fact only fifty-six per cent, against the Republicans' forty per cent. The latter was not a bad result for a party that had been in power for a generation and which was blamed for all the misdeeds of politicians and civil servants in times of civil strife, reform and war. But any hope that the verdict could be reversed – that the party of Atatürk, of secularism, of the paternalistic Civil Service could be returned to power by popular acclaim – was to be dispelled in subsequent years.

One reason was perhaps that the paternalistic Republican People's Party could preach change from above, but could not attract the new men that change produced. And after the war change was rapid. There was a further population explosion: from 17,890,000 in 1945 to 20,947,000 in 1950, 24,065,000 in 1955 and then to 27,830,000 in 1960, when the annual rate of increase reached almost three per cent. The growth of cities exceeded that of the population as a whole. In 1950 twenty-two Turks out of a hundred lived in towns, in 1960 the figure was twenty-nine out of a hundred. In the ten years which followed the end of the war, the area under cultivation was almost doubled. In absolute figures the national income was trebled between 1945 and 1960. Change brought a vast increase in the number of literate Turks: they formed twenty-two per cent of the population in 1940, forty per cent in 1960. The number of students (in schools and universities) was trebled to over three million. Change brought tension. There were the economic bottlenecks – inflation and a shortage of foreign currency. Prices increased by 100 per cent between 1950 and 1958, foreign trade deficits, accumulated between 1950 and 1960, amounted to over 1,250 million dollars. There were social bottlenecks in housing (with over two million people living in shanties in the middle 1960s), in education (with schools and universities introducing two-shift and even three-shift working), in medicine. Finally, there were political bottlenecks: authoritarianism re-emerged first on behalf of the new men and then of the old paternalistic groups, which staged a brief comeback in 1960. Change was uneven. In the economy there was a period of rapid expansion from 1950 to 1953, then slower growth until 1958, followed by stabilization. Renewed growth began cautiously in the early 1960s, reaching boom proportions in 1966.

In politics, the bright dawn of freedom in 1950 was soon clouded over. Repressive measures were taken in 1954, strengthened in 1956, and then tightened still further, until the dissatisfaction of the opponents of the regime erupted in the coup of 1960, which ushered in a brief period of military rule. Even though progress was uneven, it was never reversed: the national income continued to grow, industries developed, the ground was prepared for the introduction of new scientific techniques in agriculture. Restrictions and coups should not obscure the fact that the general elections of 1950, 1954, 1957, 1961 and 1965 were all essentially free. The concept of the popular will was being transformed from a presumption to a reality. But the popular will was not satisfied, and with good reason, since for the majority life remained hard. In absolute terms, Turkey, although richer, was still a poor country. In relative terms it was the poorest country in Europe. By Middle Eastern standards it had done remarkably well, but it was on Europe that Atatürk had set his sights – Atatürk and the entire educated class. Their common aim was to reach the standard of European civilization. The trouble was, of course, that that standard kept rising, at least as far as material goods were concerned, so that the goal of Turkish endeavours kept receding. The Western world's impact was not limited to the provision of a standard of comparison and a distant target. Ottoman reforms and the emergence of a national Turkish state were Turkish reactions to the impact of Western civilization; the development of republican Turkey in the years that followed the Second World War was largely conditioned by Western and particularly American policy.

The Truman Doctrine, proclaimed in March 1947, was the West's first official sponsorship of Turkey's development. The United States Congress began by voting 150 million dollars to help Turkey. The help was at first largely military, although Congress also authorized the despatch to Turkey of American civilian experts 'to assist in the tasks of reconstruction'. Also, military aid had long-term civilian uses. In the fifteen years which followed the end of the war, the country's road network was extended from 25,000 to 38,000 miles, and the quality of the main roads, most of which had been little better than rough tracks, improved beyond recognition. This was by no means an all-American achievement, but the Americans were the original moving force.

In July 1948 American economic aid was extended and made more systematic with the Marshall Plan. It was American aid, later supplemented by West European credits, that allowed Turkey, year after year, to import more than it exported. The sums involved, modest at first, soon began to build up: some $923 million were dispensed by 1961, $1,383 million by 1965. It was meant to be, and to some extent was, pump-priming aid, designed to secure self-generating growth. Although it covered only a fraction of the work undertaken in Turkey in the post-war years, without Western aid, progress would have been limited to what the country could afford, which, judging by the economic record of the Atatürk era, was not very much. On the other hand, forced growth meant that the development of society did not keep pace with the development and accumulation of hardware.

The election to power of the Democratic Party in May 1950 created a favourable impression in the West, particularly in the United States. Turkey was proclaimed a true democracy; its government believed in free enterprise; its opposition played the game, since it supported a national foreign policy, and respected the verdict of the electorate. When the Democratic Party government, formed by Adnan Menderes, decided only a few weeks after its election to power to send a Turkish contingent to defend South Korea, the opposition approved in

74

principle. Whether Inönü would have been so ready to help had he remained in power, is another matter: he was by nature a cautious man. Certainly Menderes' decision to rally to the United Nations flag increased Turkey's prestige in the West; certainly it was popular at home, where the war seemed a continuation of a perfectly natural struggle against 'infidel, red Muscovites'. The Turkish contribution to the defence of South Korea was real: in all, some 30,000 Turks took part in the campaign over three years. They fought well and suffered considerable casualties: over seven hundred dead and two thousand wounded. The Korean policy of the new Menderes government certainly helped it in its efforts to gain admission to the North Atlantic Treaty Organization. It was an aim which Menderes shared with Inönü and his Republican People's Party, but while Inönü had failed to achieve it before 1950, Menderes secured full membership in February 1952. The country was jubilant – Turkey was now a full member of the Western club with which it had had a love-hate relationship for generations.

For four years – between 1950 and 1954 – everything seemed to be going well. The government was popular at home and within the Western Alliance. Turkey became a member of NATO, of the Organization of European Economic Cooperation and of the Council of Europe; in February 1953 the Balkan Pact was signed with Greece and Yugoslavia; in 1951 a Treaty of Friendship was concluded with Pakistan, a treaty which in 1955 became the Baghdad Pact, grouping Turkey, Persia and Iraq, as well as Pakistan. At home, three bumper harvests in 1951, 1952 and 1953, as well as an increase of a third in the area under cultivation between 1950 and 1954, suggested that Turkey might become one of the world's major grain-exporting countries, precisely at a time when the Korean war had led to the stock-piling and, consequently, to an increase in the prices of commodities. The rise in domestic prices was still within reasonable limits – only ten per cent between 1950 and 1953. Little wonder that in the elections of 1954 the Democrats increased their share of the poll from fifty-six per cent to fifty-eight per cent, winning 504 out of the 541 seats in the Assembly.

If between 1950 and 1954 everything seemed to go right, between 1954 and 1960 most things went wrong. The surface manifestations of trouble were political, but the roots of trouble could be traced through economic failure to social inadequacy. The main political issues were the freedom of the press, the independence of the Civil Service, the judiciary, the universities and broadcasting, and the absence of constitutional checks on the legislative power of the parliamentary majority. These issues were thrown into prominence by the Menderes government's increasing impatience of criticism. Impatience led to repressive measures. Journalists could be, and thirty-five of them were, imprisoned on charges of publishing false reports, or reports likely to lead to a breach of peace. When confronted with such an accusation, they could not plead fair comment or justification. This last provision existed before the Democrats had come to power, and, as a whole, the press was freer under them than it had been in the single-party era. The same applied to public service institutions: the Civil Service, the judiciary, the universities and broadcasting had never enjoyed complete autonomy. Nevertheless, the Democrats voted themselves the power to retire judges and professors after twenty-five years of service and to suspend and retire civil servants; this went beyond the powers which the Republican People's Party possessed or needed to possess. That party, while authoritarian by nature, could generally rely on the consensus of the educated class, composed mainly of civil servants who were equally authoritarian in their dealings with the public at large. The Democrats, on the other hand, represented groups and individuals who were outside the traditional republican establishment. The repressive measures which they took were all the more resented since they were directed against people who were used to being the agents and not the objects of repression. This conflict between the establishment-in-opposition and the outsiders-in-power might not have become so acute if the establishment had not been hit in its pockets by inflation.

Economic failure also attracted to the old establishment a number of malcontents beyond the range of its traditional retainers – the state's friends in the country at large and the state's serfs in the more backward areas. The Democratic Party which faced the establishment was a coalition of discontented outsiders, but it never succeeded in grouping all of them under its wing. It was obviously the most powerful party, but it was haunted by the fear of losing its absolute majority and,

76

therefore, its power, to an unnatural coalition of the establishment and of outside splinter groups. To exorcise this fear the Democrats twice changed the electoral law in order to make electoral coalitions impossible. Thanks to these amendments, they retained power in the 1957 election, although their share of the poll fell from fifty-eight to forty-eight per cent. Conversely, the fear that admittedly small adjustments in the rules of the game would keep them forever away from power, pushed Inönü and his Republicans into militancy, which led inevitably to a head-on clash with the government and thus to an army coup. This was justified on the grounds that it was needed to separate the combatants. The Democrats moved desperately, in the weeks of student disorders before the coup, to establish an extraordinary Parliamentary Commission to investigate the opposition – a kind of Star Chamber – and proclaimed martial law in the main cities. This attempt to use the parliamentary majority in a quasi-judicial function was officially held after the coup to have violated the constitutional principle of separation of powers. It was thus on a charge of violating the Constitution that the leaders of the Democrats were convicted and that three of them – the Prime Minister Adnan Menderes, the Foreign Minister Fatin Rüştü Zorlu, and the Minister of Finance Hasan Polatkan – were hanged in September 1961 after a long political trial.

Thus, while the Democratic Party remained to the end a broadly based popular organization, it was impatience of criticism and fear of losing an overall majority that were the proximate causes of its downfall. Criticism was inevitably largely personal, but it was effective where it coincided with the economic grievances of impatient groups of electors.

Economic failure had, as we mentioned, its familiar twin manifestations: inflation and chronic shortage of foreign exchange. The price index which had risen by only ten points between 1950 and 1953, in spite of the Korean war, then climbed steeply, gaining another seventy points by 1958. In foreign trade, bad harvests and the fall in commodity prices after the end of the Korean war, reduced export earnings from almost $400 million in 1953 to less than $250 million in 1958. Although foreign credits were still available, imports had to be cut drastically from a peak of over $550 million in 1952 to $315 million in 1958. Shortages developed and with them a black market in imported goods. A system of licensing led to the usual accusations of corruption and favouritism. With the free market rate for the Turkish pound (lira) plummeting down from the official parity of nine liras to the dollar to as little as fifteen liras per dollar, any official allocation of foreign exchange at the official rate meant inordinately large profits for the recipient. The Menderes administration was accused of having caused the crisis by excessive investments and a failure to plan and coordinate them. Certainly the rate of investment increased from year to year until 1958 (from sixteen per cent of all state expenditure in 1950 to thirty-two per cent in 1957), while the budgetary deficit was allowed to grow from TL48 million to TL196 million in the same period. Persistence in a policy of growth was certainly a mistake, but it was a mistake desperately easy to make, if not inevitable, in an underdeveloped country, particularly by a democratic government bent on satisfying the aspirations of the electorate. The government's philosophy was, in any case, that debts were a temporary burden, and might with luck be written off, while the acquisition of hardware – dams, factories and roads – was a permanent gain for the country. What was not realized was that Turkish under-development was the result more of a backward social structure than of lack of industrial installations.

In agriculture, the mainstay of the Turkish economy, the change from extensive, exploitative cultivation to intensive agriculture was not achieved. While the area cultivated was increased at the expense of pasture lands and forests, yields per acre remained stationary. An increase in the number of tractors from almost nil to over 40,000 did not help; deep ploughing and the extension of cultivation to marginal hill land soon created a dust bowl in central Anatolia. Tractors arrived before soil conservation techniques were learned. There was too little irrigation and an almost total absence of artificial fertilizers, while even natural manure was more often than not burnt as fuel. Technical and entrepreneurial skills, which were almost totally absent in agriculture, were also in short supply in the rest of the economy. Tourism, which primed economic development in Italy, Spain and Greece, languished through lack of state investment and, more important, of private enterprise. The shift in the pattern of Western taste – from dry fruit to fresh and canned fruit and vegetables, from Turkish to Virginian

78

tobacco – was hardly noticed by Turkish producers and exporters. Cotton was the only new important export commodity, and here, too, quality suffered from lack of irrigation. Handling, grading and marketing techniques remained primitive. Throughout the country, the lack of technical education and under-capitalization kept productivity down. In state contracts, foreign trade, production, there was far too little competition.

It would be wrong to suggest that in all these areas there was no progress in the years of economic expansion under Menderes. But as the availability, first of an unused potential and then of foreign credits compensated for structural inadequacies, structural change was not forced on the country until after 1958. In that year, Turkey's foreign creditors persuaded the Menderes government to call a halt and apply a so-called stabilization programme. Before this programme could achieve any results – which it eventually did – the Menderes government was overthrown on 27 May 1960.

Once again political, economic and social factors were involved. Political repression and the burden placed by inflation on salaried classes followed by the general discomfort of deflation, had taken their toll of Menderes' supporters. Perhaps more important was the challenge to the establishment from the new men, symbolized by the ward chairmen of the Democratic Party. Half-educated, half-westernized, but usually self-confident and arrogant, they came from small market towns, shanties, and poorer districts in the larger cities, to give Menderes his electoral majority and ask, in return, for protection from the bureaucracy. For the first time in the history of the Republic an alternative structure of power and influence had been constructed, challenging the power of the bureaucracy. The bureaucratic establishment feared and hated it. The extent of these emotions became obvious at the trials of the deposed leadership. It was fear, the establishment's fear of the sans-culottes that killed Menderes.

1, 2　The Mosque of Süleyman the Magnificent was built by the Sultan's architect, Sinan, in 1556. Modelled on the great sixth-century Byzantine church Santa Sophia, also in Istanbul, its dome is 174 feet high and 86 feet in diameter. The sign between the minarets proclaims 'Republic'; below, a sixteenth-century woodcut by Melchior Lorch shows how little the mosque has changed.

3, 4   Süleyman I, known as the Magnificent in the West and the Lawgiver in Turkey, ruled the Empire for forty-six years. Most of his conquests were in the West. During his reign, Turkey became a major sea power, led by his admiral, Hayrettin Barbaros (right).

5   The capital of the Seljuk Empire was Konya, where one of Turkey's oldest mosques, Alâettin Camii (thirteenth century), still serves as a place of worship.

6, 7, 8 Traditions of East and West meet in Turkey: above, the *mevlevi* or whirling order of dervishes founded by the mystic poet Jalaluddin Rumi; on the Mediterranean shores, the Theatre of Aspendos dating from the second century AD, one of the finest Roman ruins in the Middle East; in Bodrum, the classical Halicarnassus, a castle (below right) built by the Knights of St John at Rhodes at the beginning of the fifteenth century and captured by Süleyman the Magnificent in 1522.

9, 10, 11, 12 Four Presidents of the Republic. Above left: Mustafa Kemal (Atatürk), founder and architect of modern Turkey. When he died in 1938, Ismet Inönü (above right) became the second President, having been Prime Minister under Atatürk. As the leader of the opposition against the Democratic party, Inönü favoured the 27 May Revolution which deposed Adnan Menderes (below left), and resulted in his hanging. Cemal Gürsel (below right) was President between 1961 and 1966.

13, 14   Gallipoli, site of the famous First World War campaign, where Allied troops failed in bloody battles to force the Straits and open the way to Istanbul. It was at Gallipoli that Mustafa Kemal (Atatürk) first became famous as an outstanding commander. Below, the bloodless 27 May Revolution, where crowds and troops gathered in Ankara to celebrate the deposition of the Menderes government. The 1960 coup was celebrated as a return to the principles of Atatürk, to rule by the establishment.

15 Adequate medical
facilities are still one of
Turkey's major problems,
particularly in country
regions. Here social welfare
workers, conducting a surv
ascertain the medical histor
of a village family.

16 Seventy-two per cent o
Turkey's population is
engaged in agriculture.
Racks of tobacco, the secon
largest export crop.

17 Women peasants
pick cotton, now the
leading export crop. Major
advances in irrigation and
fertilization have increased
the production of cotton by
more than a third in four
years.

Despite considerable
progress, most farmers still
rely on the more primitive ox
and cart to transport their
crops. However, in recent
years the tractor and other
modern farm machinery have
been increasing use.

Turkey's major fishing
industry is centred in the Sea
of Marmara and the Bosporus.
Bonito, tunny, swordfish,
mackerel, herring and sardines
constitute the catch. Efforts
are being made to increase
exports of fishery products.

Turkey also exports
much of its precious olive oil,
using imported or domestic
vegetable oils for the
manufacture of margarine.
Here Turkish women and
children beat sunflowers for
oil.

21 This farmer lives in the arid, wild region of Central Anatolia where the landscape is populated by fantastic shapes formed by volcanic tufa. Many have been made into dwellings; others, formerly chapels, house some of the finest Byzantine frescoes extant.

6   The new nation

THE 1960 COUP WAS CARRIED OUT by the armed forces to
the unanimous applause of the educated classes. It was hailed as a return
to the principles of Atatürk. And in a way the description was
appropriate – for it was a return to rule by the establishment, to a
unitary structure of power, to authoritarianism.

In the countryside, the political village headman was replaced by the
school teacher; everywhere party ward organizations were disbanded.
A new constitution brought in a host of checks against the power of the
majority: proportional representation, a Second Chamber of university
graduates (only university graduates may stand for elections to the
Turkish Senate), a Constitutional Court with powers to invalidate
legislation, entrenched rights and autonomous institutions. The
establishment had developed a social conscience, or perhaps its more
intelligent members saw that socialism was now the only possible
justification for authoritarianism. It was, however, to be socialism
imposed by the sons of Atatürk's officials, and the grandsons of
Ottoman *pashas* and *beys*, who had been assimilated into the
establishment.

The 1960 revolution was neither extreme nor consistent. It was
presented to the people as a restoration not only of clean government but
also of freedom and many, if not most of its leaders, were honourable
men who meant to carry out their promises. Those who did not –
fourteen radical members of the revolutionary junta – were purged in
November 1960 and thereafter, except for the senseless severity of the
verdicts on Democratic Party leaders, moderate counsels prevailed and
the country was guided back to parliamentary rule. A new constitution
was drawn up and endorsed by a small majority at a properly conducted

Map of modern Turkey

referendum. Free elections were held in October 1961. Although the Democratic Party was disbanded, other parties of a similar character were soon formed. It took, however, some time before one of them, the Justice Party, emerged as the main successor of the Democratic Party. In the meantime, the fragmentation of the anti-establishment vote allowed the armed forces to impose a compromise within the constitutional framework. General Gürsel, the official leader, although not the moving spirit of the 27 May Revolution, was elected President. Ismet Inönü became Prime Minister of a government which included his own Republicans as well as the Justice Party. The coalition was assured of a big paper majority: the Republican People's Party had polled thirty-five per cent of the vote (significantly less than in 1957) and won 173 seats out of 450 in the Assembly; the Justice Party with thirty-five per cent of the poll, had 158 seats. The coalition was widely and perhaps rightly described as unnatural. It was a daring and a promising experiment, grouping for the first time the establishment and its enemies, the old men and the new men, or, to give them their misleading Turkish labels, the progressives and the reactionaries. This first coalition government lasted only seven months – long enough, however, to prove that parliamentary rule was what the country and the majority of the armed forces really wanted. In February 1962 the Commandant of the Military Academy in Ankara, a Colonel Aydemir, tried his hand at a coup and failed. With the temper of the armed forces still uncertain, Inönü preferred to conciliate the enemies of the constitution by granting a full pardon to the rebels.

In June 1962 the coalition formula was varied: the Justice Party withdrew into opposition and was replaced by three smaller anti-establishment parties. The second coalition worked better and lasted longer than the first. It secured parliamentary approval of and, much more significantly, the consent of the armed forces to the release of many imprisoned leaders of the now dissolved Democratic Party. It launched the first post-war Five Year Plan for development and obtained enough foreign credits for the purpose. In May 1963 it defeated a second attempt by Colonel Aydemir to overthrow the constitution. The coup was a dismal failure, and, as opinion in the country was clearly shown to be against revolutionary adventures, the government felt itself strong

92

enough to prosecute the rebels. The unfortunate Colonel Aydemir and his chief lieutenant were hanged, with hardly a voice raised in protest. However, while the second coalition was battling to defend the constitution, the Justice Party was waxing strong in opposition. Reflation had not yet started in earnest; life for the majority of the people was hard; establishment paternalism, though muted, was still resented. The government had time for one more important measure: in July 1963 strikes were made legal for the first time in Turkish history. Then in November, local elections showed that the Justice Party had almost completed the job of gathering in the anti-establishment vote. It polled forty-four per cent of all the votes cast, against the Republicans' thirty-seven per cent. The small anti-establishment parties thereupon decided to follow the example of the Justice Party. They left the coalition, allowing İnönü to form a minority government on the understanding that the electoral law would be changed to their advantage. This opposition posture did not help the small parties. In the Senate elections, held in June 1964, the Justice Party's share of the poll increased to fifty per cent. The fact that the death on the eve of the elections of the Party's first leader, General Gümüşpala, did not effect the result, showed how little political persuasions in the country had to do with personalities.

In February 1965, the small parties, having failed to prosper either in alliance with the Republicans or in opposition, joined forces with the Justice Party in an anti-establishment coalition headed by a neutral Prime Minister, Senator Ürgüplü. The Ürgüplü government proved that the armed forces were willing to allow the successors of Menderes to take office and it opened the way to the Justice Party's victory in the general elections in October 1965. In spite of a new electoral law favouring small parties, the Justice Party, under its new leader Süleyman Demirel, won the absolute majority of seats in both Chambers and proceeded to form the government.

The wheel had come full circle in five years. But of course the country had not stood still in the interim. The armed forces had emerged as a powerful pressure group. Many members of the establishment lost hope of ever achieving power through the ballot box and began to favour authoritarian solutions under a general socialist banner. Economically, the years of deflation from 1958 to 1963 were, in fact, a period of slow progress. Industrialization continued, the more efficient enterprises prospered, private enterprise tried to fight its way through difficulties. The peasants showed initiative by moving to the towns or even further afield to Western Europe, where for the first time, Turkish emigrant workers made their appearance. In the towns, employment in industry increased, but not enough to absorb all the unemployed. Attempting to widen their appeal, the establishment party of state paternalism and secularism added to its armoury the powerful weapon of xenophobia in the guise of anti-Americanism.

The growth of anti-Americanism was helped by the development of the Cyprus problem. Until 1960, Cyprus had been an anachronism – while the populations of all other Ottoman lands had been sorted out by nationality, with the few remaining national minorities clearly subordinated to the will of the majority, in British-ruled Cyprus 100,000 Turks could hold their own against four times their number of Greeks. Greek nationalists had never been content with the situation, and in the 'fifties made one of their periodic attempts to dislodge the British. Only this time, with British imperial resolve all but gone, the attempt was clearly going to be successful. Equally clearly, the substitution of Greek for British rule would make second-class citizens of the Turkish Cypriots. There was, therefore, nothing surprising or immoral in their attempt, seconded by the Turkish government, to gain control over their destiny. But since oppression of national minorities is the rule in all developing countries, it was obviously going to be difficult to establish an exception in the case of the Cypriot Turks.

The Menderes government took on this difficult, if not impossible task both for internal political reasons and because of a misreading of history. It argued that in Ottoman times when Turks had been lost to alien rule, it was because the Empire had been backward and 'oriental'. Now that Turkey was progressive and was accepted as a 'Western' state, it should be able to protect its kinsmen abroad. It was an argument that sounded strange at a time when thousands of Westerners were being handed over by progressive governments at home to be ruled by backward majorities in dark continents. Nevertheless, a militant Turkish policy, coupled with a measure of British sympathy, seemed at first to have achieved success. Just before his overthrow, Menderes and

94

the Greek Prime Minister Karamanlis agreed on a constitution for an independent Cyprus in which the Turks were to enjoy complete self-rule and even a privileged status. This status could, however, be maintained only by the external application of Turkish strength to hold steady the balance of forces in the island. In December 1963, when the Cypriot Greeks attempted to force a change in the constitution, the Inönü government in Ankara hesitated to apply that strength. Within a few weeks the opportunity was lost. British and then United Nations troops were called in to maintain not the old, but perforce the new *status quo*, with the Turks now beleaguered in a few enclaves, as their ancestors had been in Oczacow on the Danube, in Tripoli in the Peloponnese, Belgrade, Plevna and elsewhere during the years of Ottoman retreat.

In the early phase of the Cyprus problem – between 1954 and 1960 – Turkish resentment had been vented mildly on the British and much more visibly on the Greeks. In September 1955 anti-Greek feeling, whipped up by the government, erupted in riots in Istanbul. Greek churches and property were sacked, but there were no casualties. After 1963 order in Istanbul was preserved, anti-Greek feeling finding satisfaction in the deportation of Greek nationals. The 50,000 or so Greeks with Turkish citizenship were, however, left undisturbed. Abroad, it was this time the Americans who were blamed for standing in the way of Turkish rights, particularly after June 1964 when strong American warnings induced the Inönü government to call off an invasion of Cyprus. Political anti-Americanism – the feeling, that is, that the Americans had not repaid in Cyprus the debt which they had incurred to the Turks in Korea and for Turkish services in the Atlantic Alliance – was reinforced by economic anti-Americanism. Before 1960, particularly in Democratic Party circles, there were complaints that America was not giving enought help to Turkey; more precisely, that America had refused to come to the aid of Menderes when he had to call off his development programme in 1958. American reluctance to present the Menderes government with an open cheque coincided with Soviet moves to woo Turkey away from the West. Immediately after Stalin's death, in July 1953, the Soviet government officially withdrew the demands which it had advanced in 1945. Soon afterwards came offers of Soviet technical and financial aid for industrial development. At first Turkey turned a deaf ear to these proposals, but in 1960 Menderes decided to visit Moscow. However, he was overthrown immediately afterwards by the army and it was left to his successors to take the first tentative steps in securing normal relations with the northern neighbour.

Complaints of inadequate Western aid continued after the 1960 revolution but with less conviction. Aid was, in fact, considerably stepped up, particularly after a fourteen-nation Aid to Turkey Consortium was formed in 1962. With the Consortium, not only Western government aid, but also Western private investments increased, and this increase gave rise to a different sort of complaint. It was now argued that foreigners were taking possession of Turkey, that Western aid was a disguise for capitalist penetration and exploitation. But while criticism of the extent of aid had been general and was, if anything, voiced more often by people outside the establishment whose standard of living was, after all, rising only very slowly, criticism of aid as such came from the old establishment and its supporters, from people whose status was threatened by the rise of free enterprise in the country. In 1964 and 1965 the peaks of political and economic xenophobia coincided. Frustration over Cyprus reinforced frustration over the rise not only of capitalism but also of a technological society. At the same time, Russian endeavours which had been pursued since 1954, were beginning to have some effect. As the establishment moved left, however, the majority of the people moved right, away from paternalism. While xenophobic propaganda was not without effect, the old conviction of the establishment that 'civilization' was to be found in the West gained more converts among the rising lower middle class than it lost among the old-style intellectuals.

This conviction, which was fully shared by the Justice Party government, formed in 1965 by Süleyman Demirel, did not prevent the emergence of a new look in Turkish foreign policy. The new look could justly be described as one of greater independence. But this was not an exclusively Turkish phenomenon: greater freedom of manoeuvre was the result of the ending of the Cold War and not of any sudden decision to put Turkish national interests first. All Turkish governments had naturally put Turkish interests first. Mustafa Kemal's decision to make use of Soviet Russian help in the Anatolian campaign, his subsequent *rapprochement* with the Western democracies, the treaties of alliance with Britain and France no less than the non-aggression treaty with Nazi Germany, Inönü's grateful acceptance of the Truman Doctrine, and the decision of Menderes to fight in Korea and to seek membership of NATO, the careful steps to test the intentions of Stalin's successors – steps taken by Menderes, Inönü, Ürgüplü and Demirel – all these moves were inspired not by quixotic impulses, but by sober calculations of national interest. There were, of course, shifts of emphasis in the appraisal of the national interest; there were also mistakes. For most of the time the emphasis was on the defence of the national territory; then gradually the feeling of insecurity, for which there was every historical justification, lessened and internal development came to dominate calculations of the national interest. If it were not for the problem posed fortuitously by the Turkish minority in Cyprus – and the decision to save that minority from the prevailing tide in world affairs – this new trend would perhaps have been seen more clearly.

But neither foreign nor home policies can be discussed only in terms of impersonal trends and forces. The personalities of the leading statesmen also left a clear mark: Inönü first, the careful heir to Ottoman traditions of statecraft, a man who knew how to divide his enemies, and, as a precautionary measure, his friends. His main contribution to Turkish history was his firm decision in 1947 that paternalism had had its day. His successor as President, Celâl Bayar, came to lead the enemies of the establishment largely as a result of his rivalry with Inönü in the last days of Atatürk. He was undoubtedly courageous, but too unyielding, and his influence on his Prime Minister, Menderes, seems to have been disastrous. Menderes himself, with his charm, his inexperience, even his emotional instability, mirrored the character of the country's rising new men – naïvely over-simplifying the processes of development, obsessed with industrial hardware around them and consumer durables at home, but lacking both the virtues and the vices of an acquisitive and painstaking middle class. His boast that he would create a millionaire in every neighbourhood was ridiculed by his critics, but represented the dream of a naïve society, which was freeing itself from the straitjacket of paternalism. Paternalism – of a conservative and almost kindly sort – was represented by the two successive military presidents elected after the 27 May Revolution – Generals Gürsel and Sunay. In the eyes of the majority they enjoyed the advantage of not being intellectuals. They could therefore be trusted to show some respect for traditional values. Finally, Süleyman Demirel, the man who made the second attempt to work a free-enterprise economic miracle in Turkey, symbolized a new stage in Turkey's evolution: he was the son of a peasant, where Menderes had been the son of a landowner; he was a trained engineer, where Menderes had held a tenuous legal degree; he knew the West by personal experience, not by repute. He was one of the 'new men', whereas Menderes had miraculously identified himself with the new men, without being one of them. He was the first entre-preneur to lead a Turkish government. For a nation that consisted traditionally of soldiers, civil servants and peasants, it was a new experience and a measure of the change it had undergone.

7 The people: unity and diversity

AT THE TIME of the 1965 census there were, in round figures, 31,400,000 people living in Turkey. The preponderant majority of them were, by any reckoning, Turks – in other words they spoke Turkish and were Muslims. This Turkish majority can be subdivided in different ways: it can be classified for example into local Turks or, to use a Turkish expression, 'the children of Anatolia', and the refugees and sons of refugees. As we have seen, just as Anatolia had been a reservoir of Turkish colonizers in the years of Ottoman expansion, so it became a shelter for Muslim refugees in the centuries of defeat and decline. In the last pre-war census, roughly one million, of a population which then stood at sixteen million, were foreign-born. Since the war there has been one fresh wave of immigration when Turkey had to find room for 200,000 Turks whom the Communist authorities forced out of Bulgaria. The refugees brought originally their own national languages or dialects and distinctive ways of life. Circassians, Abkhazes, Crimean, and to a lesser extent Volga Tartars, Slav-speaking Bosnian and Bulgarian Muslims, Greek-speaking Cretan Muslims, Albanians, 'Roumelians' (Turkish-speaking refugees from the Balkans), Dönmes or descendants of converted Jews, could be distinguished alongside indigenous groups such as Lazes, Arabs and Kurds. To suggest that these groups have all been absorbed would be to overstate the case. But with the possible exception of the Kurds and the border Arabs, they are being absorbed. They have become or are becoming Turks, because they or their ancestors have chosen Turkey. They have enriched the country with their diversity and not introduced new divisions into it.

The case of the Kurds or the Arabs is, at least potentially, different. There is for them an alternative focus of allegiance. Their number is difficult to determine: Turkish statistics which showed that in 1960 6·7 per cent of the population had Kurdish and 1·3 per cent had Arabic for their mother tongue probably underestimate the true figures. The Arabs are concentrated south of the Taurus mountains. They are mainly to be found in the province of Hatay (formerly the Sandjak of Alexandretta), but there are also groups of Arab peasants, tribesmen, and, in some cases, townsmen in Çukurova (Cilicia) to the west, and the provinces of Urfa, Gaziantep, Mardin, Malatya, Diyarbakır and Siirt to the east. They are to some extent balanced by small Turkish communities scattered through northern Syria and Iraq.

The Kurds are a much more important group or collection of groups. They are concentrated largely in the eastern and south-eastern parts of Turkey. In some provinces: Hakkâri in the extreme southeast, the mountains of Dersim (province of Tunçeli), Ağrı (Ararat province) they form the majority of the population. In many places they have replaced the Armenians and Assyrians who were ejected in the First World War. The Kurds are or were essentially a mountain people, organized in tribes, many of them nomadic. In the past they gave their allegiance to tribal lay and religious leaders, the two functions being often combined in one person. They speak a number of dialects – which are usually but not invariably mutually intelligible. However, as elsewhere in Turkey, Kurdish society is changing: nomads are settling, tribal organization is breaking down, the old leaders are giving way to a new élite of professional men, most of them trained in the universities of Istanbul and Ankara. Often, perhaps in the majority of cases, a Kurd receiving higher education in Turkey chooses to become a Turk. But there are some who find Kurdish nationalism appealing, although even they do not at present ask for more than a measure of autonomy and, in the first place, official recognition of their language (an Indo-European language akin to Persian) and culture. Kurdish nationalists are a minority among Turkish Kurds, but then nationalists almost always start as minorities. Whether they will be able to convince or coerce the majority of Turkish Kurds to choose Kurdish nationalism remains an open question.

The first obstacle that Kurdish (or other) nationalists have to overcome are the cohesive bonds of religion. As Muslims, Kurds and Arabs were not aliens, but full citizens of a state that was until a generation ago officially an Islamic one, and that is still so conceived by people who do not know better. For in spite of official secularism, religion is still for the majority of the inhabitants of Turkey the main source of their identity and the criterion of differentiation between them and foreigners. Islam is the religion of ninety-nine per cent of the country, and only in the case of some members of the educated élite has it become a meaningless entry on an identity card. In the villages, where two-thirds of the population live, religious observance is almost universal. This does not, of course, mean that all the precepts of Islam are observed: while pork is always avoided like the plague, alcoholic drink (which is equally illicit in Islam) is seldom refused and, usually, positively welcomed. In the villages, attendance at mosque once a week is the rule, in a medium-sized town it has been put at a quarter of the male population. But even there, most men go to a mosque on Fridays during the month of fasting of Ramadan.[24] In a wider sense, the religion of Islam provides almost all the points of reference of a villager's life. In towns, where the demands of technology no less than secularist legislation have visibly altered people's way of life, the influence of religion is more circumscribed and elusive. Just below the agnostic élite, it is reduced to little more than a vague belief in God and in many, perhaps most cases, an unneurotic acceptance of things-as-they-are as the will of God. This acceptance is not tantamount to fatalism in the sense of resignation. A Turkish sociologist was surprised when seventy-nine per cent of her sample in a small Anatolian town answered affirmatively to the question: 'Do you agree that if we are sufficiently resolute no obstacle can turn us from our path?' Her surprise arose from the fact that sixty-eight per cent of the same sample, when asked, 'What is the cause of death?' replied, 'God's will.'[25] Yet the two positions are perfectly consistent in Islam, as in most other religions. Acceptance of the 'datum', of the circumstances to which the human person reacts in so far as it can, is crucial to Islam and it is because of the survival of this psychological attitude among people who have ceased to be Muslims in a formal sense, that one can say that there is often more religion in a Turkish agnostic than in a Western believer.

As in other basically religious societies, attacks on religion, or, more politely, on 'superstition, conservatism, political partisanship, reaction, exploitation (or what have you) masquerading as religion' are a feature of the Turkish intellectual scene. Only in Turkey the usual psycho-logical conflict, the usual revolt against feelings, in oneself and others, which one can explain but cannot conjure away, has been exacerbated by secularist authoritarianism. Thus, while religion has been re-introduced into the curricula of primary and middle schools (against vocal secularist opposition), there is no provision for the religious education or, much more important, the expression of the religious feelings of adolescents – no religious education, prayers, mosques or places of worship – in high schools or universities. As a result, where adolescent religious enthusiasm is not replaced by its mirror image – secularist and, currently, socialist enthusiasm associated with the Atatürk cult, it is diverted, at best, into the banned dervish fraternities and at worst into a nationalism, misnamed 'traditionalist' to distinguish it from 'progressive, socialist nationalism', but in fact radical and often racialist in character. One curious feature is that the 'progressives' are usually socially superior to the 'traditionalists', so that a government of anti-establishment parties brings 'traditionalists' to the fore. The rising importance and even the rise to power of a new lower middle class, can thus be represented as a revival of Islamic reaction. The accusation that the Justice Party stood for religious reaction, that it could not even be trusted to protect the republican form of government, was officially voiced by Ismet Inönü in the campaign preceding the mid-term Senate elections held in June 1966. When election results showed that the Justice Party had once again increased its share of the poll – this time to fifty-seven per cent – Inönü commented that religious reaction was clearly even stronger than he had supposed. Reaction is a vague word. There is no doubt that the majority of the Turkish people desire economic progress through industrialization, a more efficient and also a more considerate administration and greater freedom. These are not reactionary ambitions. The restoration of the Caliphate and of the *sharia* are simply no longer relevant to the hopes of people whose way of life is daily becoming more remote from the tenets of the Holy Law of Islam. Nevertheless, a certain degree of Islamic reverence, of respect, and even of nostalgia for the Muslim religion as a way of life, does represent the moral aspect, or perhaps self-justification of the search for material advancement. The revolt against authoritarianism has not been confined to any one field. While in the economy there has been a reaction against state capitalism, in the administration there has been a revulsion against bureaucratic arbitrariness, and in general behaviour a demand for a modicum of respect for the religious feelings of the majority. On religious holidays most Turks expect their official leaders to express on their behalf the wish that God should prosper them. This expectation is resented by the old establishment as an impudent denial of the secularist state which, however, through the Department of Religious Affairs controls all religious appointments. Completely consistent secularism is, of course, as impossible to realize in Turkey as anywhere else, and the more freedom is won by the Turks the more their state will reflect their religious feelings and susceptibilities. In the last resort, and particularly in the present time of rapid social and economic change, what they seek in religion is comfort and not temporal leadership. The establishment apologists argue that not only secularism, but state control over religion are needed lest the country be dragged back to the horrors of theocracy. But an industrial theocracy is so bizarre a concept that one can hardly assume that the Turks should want to see it realized in their country.

The advocates of strict secularism argue that any lessening of state control over religion would also lead to strife among Muslim sects in Anatolia. It is true that strife between the two main sects in Islam – the Sunnis and the Shiis (the latter better known in Turkey as Alevis, or followers of the Caliph Ali) – had been a feature of Anatolian history. But it had always been the result of efforts by the sultans and by the hierarchy of the *ulema* to impose Sunnism by force – a policy which is neither possible nor desired by anyone today. Moreover, the religious struggle in Anatolia was part of the political struggle between Sunni sultans in Istanbul and Shii shahs in Persia. That struggle, too, is now past history. In the present context of industrialization and the challenge of secularism, differences between Sunnis and Shiis are hardly likely to present a menace to the public order. This is also true of the other religious division in Islam – between schools or rites *among* Sunnis. Most Turks belong to the Hanefi rite, while a minority – in the south-eastern provinces, south of the Taurus – practise the Shafii rite. Although for reasons of geography, many Arabs and Kurds belong to this rite, the division between rites, just as the division between sects does not, as a whole, correspond to national divisions, and is, therefore, unlikely to harden into political antagonism.

In Turkey, as elsewhere in the Middle East, any minorities, be they national minorities like the Kurds or religious minorities, like the Shiis, are, at least potentially, apt to express their separateness and their grievances through the medium of the most extreme political grouping that may be available – which at present means Communist or crypto-Communist groupings. In Turkey this is still a minor threat for, in spite of official secularism, Islam remains as a unifying rather than a divisive force.

More important than ethnic origin and religious difference as a criterion of classification, is the clear division between town and country, urban and village Turk. Although shanty towns have emerged as a half-way house, although buses can now reach many villages, and in spite of the growth of mass communications, town and village are still different worlds. If villagers are daily migrating to towns, townsmen remain unable to live in a village for any length of time. Reformers, socialist intellectuals, progressives of all kinds fulminate against rural backwardness and exploitation, without ever leaving their flats in Istanbul and Ankara. The peasants have, of course, been exploited, but not so much by landlords and religious leaders as by the bureaucracy and by urban society in general. With cooperatives still few and far between, marketing is primitive and yields more profit to the urban middleman and retailer than to the peasant producer. Educational facilities are perforce concentrated in towns and, although education is free, few peasants can afford to board their children away beyond the fifth grade. Medical facilities in villages are almost non-existent. If the villagers are backward, it is not because of the dead weight of religious superstition. The peasants' demands for schools, medical attention, roads, piped water and electricity, cheap fertilizers and consumer goods are not reactionary demands. If they occasionally come into conflict with the schoolteacher, it is not because they reject education, but because they ask for respect for at least some of their beliefs. If they often clash with forestry officials, it is not because they resent the sight of trees, but because they cannot obtain fuel or open up new land for cultivation except by felling forests. Rural education and development have until recently been almost completely neglected. But with democracy, with the need to win votes, some progress has been made and the rate of progress is accelerating. Some peasants have shown initiative and improved their economic status. As villages develop, so social divisions within them are accentuated, but in villages as in the country at large, it is exploitation not of private man by private man but of private man by the state that causes most resentment.

Although the oppression practised by reactionary landlords is a favourite subject with left-wing writers, such figures as exist suggest that Turkish agriculture suffers from fragmentation rather than concentration of holdings. According to an agricultural census carried out in 1952, some twenty million hectares of land were worked by over two and a half million households, most of them of peasant proprietors. Large estates – over 100 hectares – covered only some fifteen per cent of the cultivated area.[26] True, concentration of land – and of power – is greater in the case of at least one cash crop, cotton. But other cash crops – sugar-beet, tea, hazelnuts, etc. – are grown mainly by small peasant proprietors. Also the landlord or *agha* (although *agha* is sometimes an honorific title given to an elder who is not appreciably richer than his neighbours) is not always considered as a local oppressor. Often he is the peasant's defender against the authorities, particularly in the Kurdish areas in the east. A decision by the revolutionary junta in 1960 to exile a number of prominent Kurdish *aghas* was widely resented by their tenants, retainers and neighbours, and had to be rescinded. However, the paternalistic *agha* is part of an old-style village community – a community which has not yet changed over to a money economy, a community whose distinguishing mark is the provision of a free guesthouse for strangers. Today more and more guesthouses are being closed, while new men – the owner-driver of the village lorry, the peasant with educated relatives in towns – are beginning to dominate the village.

Mass communications – largely in the shape of the transistor wireless – have penetrated the village. Here as in most other fields outside that of agricultural productivity, development since the war has been spectacular. In 1945 there were under 200,000 licensed wireless sets in

Turkey, in 1966 over two million (one estimate which included un-
licensed transistors put the figure at almost four million). In the medium
of the press, changes have been almost as rapid. In 1945, fifty thousand
copies was a very respectable circulation for a national newspaper. In
the middle 'sixties, the circulation of the country's most popular paper
exceeded the half million mark and was still rising rapidly. Today
there is hardly a village without a transistor and very few where at least
one copy of a newspaper does not penetrate. Advertising and initial
steps towards national distribution of consumer goods have come with
mass communications. Although it is too early to speak of a profound
change in peasant feeding and buying habits, tinned goods have made
their appearance in at least some village stores. In towns, the change has
been much more rapid and is symbolized by what may be called the
margarine revolution – margarine, almost unknown ten years ago,
having become a staple of urban diet.

There has been much discussion in Turkey to decide whether it is
desirable or even possible to foster the growth of a self-reliant middle
class. A professional middle class, although small by Western standards,
now exists and to that extent the question has been resolved. But if the
object is to create a middle class with enough economic power to avoid
leaning on the state, it is doubtful whether this object has been achieved.
While entrepreneurs could often be accused of seeking easy profits
through state favours and contracts, the state too has never freed
enterprise in any real sense. Even today the owner of one of the largest
industrial undertakings in the country can claim with justice that his
entire fortune can be swept away by an arbitrary decision taken by a
Ministry official in Ankara.

While the middle class, with its trials and its shortcomings, has
attracted attention, the emergence of a large lower-middle class has
passed almost unnoticed, except perhaps by successful newspaper
editors. Semi-traditional, semi-educated, self-reliant in some respects
while yearning for state paternalism in others, avid for material improvement and particularly for consumer durables, unprepossessing in its
tastes, this class is probably the most dynamic element in Turkish
society today. By Western standards it is, of course, poor. It has
graduated to wireless sets, newspapers, toothpaste, margarine, paraffin

heaters, some local holiday travel. But television sets and cars are still unattained by the vast majority. 'The decision whether or not to set up a television service will demonstrate whether Turkey is or is not a civilized country', a Turkish journalist wrote in the early 'sixties. Since then, in this respect too Turkey has chosen 'civilization', but most of the citizens still cannot afford it. As for private motor cars, there were less than 80,000 of them in the middle 'sixties among a population of over thirty million. And with public transport, like almost all other public services, usually inadequate and uncomfortable, the ownership of a motor car symbolized luxury and the achievement of the living standards of Western civilization.

22   Istanbul, formerly Constantinople, straddles Europe and Asia. On the
European side the Golden Horn divides the old city from the shopping centre of
Beyoglu. The Süleymaniye Mosque overlooks the meeting of the waters.

23, 24 Istanbul's great covered bazaar (left), where you can buy anything from teapots to carpets. Below, Galata Bridge, across the mouth of the Golden Horn, starting point of ferries for the Bosporus, suburbs in Asia and Princes Islands.

25, 26 Ankara (right), chosen by Atatürk to be the capital of the Republic in 1923, is now a thriving metropolis boasting some of Turkey's most advanced architecture. Izmir (below right) is the chief city of Aegean Turkey, and the country's second largest port, handling the bulk of Turkey's agricultural exports.

27–30 Turkey's varied landscape: above left, rock dwellings at Ortahisar in Central Anatolia, some of which are twenty-three storeys high. Left, sponge fishing – a dying industry – and (above right) progress in forestry at Aradanuç State Forest, Çorum. Right, wood is made into furniture in one of Istanbul's many streets where craftsmen ply their trade.

31, 32 Industry of any size started with the Republic, but its growth did not gather speed until after the Second World War. Production of iron and steel began just before the war, when Turkey's first mill was built at Karabük (above). The Sakarya, 600 kilometres long and one of Turkey's major rivers, has a large dam at Sariyar (below) and another begun in 1967, at Gökçekaya.

33, 34   Oil prospecting began in 1932, There are three refineries, at Batman, Izmit and (above) Mersin. A fourth is going up near Izmir. It is estimated that by 1970, these four refineries will produce 10 million tons of petroleum products.

Below, Istanbul's busy Haydarpaşa port.

35 The Topkapi museum, Istanbul, from the fifteenth to the nineteenth century
the home of Ottoman Sultans, now contains relics of Turkey's imperial past,
including jewellery, porcelain, arms, maps and manuscripts.

8   The society: education, culture, welfare

THROUGHOUT TURKISH SOCIETY, money and education are the main determinants of class. Essentially the same criteria applied in Ottoman society where status was determined by service – military or civil to the Islamic commonwealth and the Sultan at its head – and scholarship, primarily religious scholarship. Riches were theoretically the rewards of service, even in the case of landowners, most of whom were, again theoretically, fief-holders. In practice, too, riches usually disappeared when service terminated. If it did not revert to the Treasury, as was often the case, the rich man's property was traditionally squandered by his sons, the *mirasyedi* or 'eater of inherited fortune' being a cliché figure in Turkish society. There was thus little room for an aristocracy of birth. True the flux, and to Western eyes, the arbitrariness and impermanence of Islamic society were somewhat steadied in the nineteenth century, when the Western ideal of the inviolability of life and property was, at least officially, accepted. Nevertheless, old habits as well as the political vicissitudes of the Ottoman state, took a heavy toll of personal fortunes, and it was mainly in Ottoman lands under foreign rule, such as Egypt, Cyprus and, between the world wars, the Arab Middle East, that fortunes could be preserved or inherited, more or less intact, in spite of the disgrace or the demise of their original owner. Thus what passes today for a Turkish aristocracy has in most cases its origin in the nineteenth century. Also until recently, where an upper-class Turkish family was unusually rich, the source of the riches was more often than not outside the territory of the Turkish Republic. Descent from the nineteenth-century Ottoman Pashas and property owned in the Arab world were the two main characteristics of a tiny upper class, which was, and to some extent still is, to be seen in Istanbul. However, now that nationalism and 'revolutionary socialism' have driven out Western influence from these short-lived privileged sanctuaries in the Middle East, many of these upper-class Turkish families have reverted to norm. In other words, their fortunes have once again come to depend on personal endeavour, which usually means personal connection with the state. In the meantime some material continuity has of course been achieved within the Turkish Republic and with it have come the beginnings, but only the beginnings, of a small hereditary bourgeoisie.

Education remains the chief means to social advancement in modern Turkey. As state education is free, the door is theoretically open to all, although, as we have seen, advancement from the villages is limited by the peasants' ability to maintain their children (in minimal conditions of comfort) away from home after the age of twelve. In addition to financial limitations there are, of course, also limitations of facilities: there are not enough schools and university places available. Even so, the proportion of illiteracy, which in the middle 1960s was usually given as sixty per cent, is steadily coming down. The 1965 census showed that of the total number of Turks aged six years and above, the proportion of illiterates stood at fifty-two per cent. More important, according to official figures released in 1966, over four million children attended primary schools which could accom-modate eighty-three per cent of children of school age. One can, therefore, expect a very rapid decline in illiteracy figures. Other problems in education will be more difficult to resolve. Since in 1966 there were more than 430 pupils to each teacher in primary schools, these could hardly provide more than the simplest training in the bare elements of literacy. As against four million pupils in primary schools, there were only 800,000 in secondary schools of all kinds, 580,000 of them in three-year middle schools. The number of students in universities and colleges of higher education was 85,000. However, absolute figures can be misleading. For one thing, as in other rapidly developing countries, the rate of change is most important. The fact that in 1966, primary education was provided for eighty-three per cent of the maximum potential intake, whereas five years earlier the proportion was seventy per cent, suggests that universal primary education will be achieved before long. Similarly, the number of pupils in technical schools increased from 60,000 in 1963 to 107,000 in 1966, again suggesting a rapid growth of a technically literate class. On the other hand, numbers bear little relation to quality. Although the proportion of Turks undergoing secondary education is low by Western standards, in absolute terms the number of graduates of secondary schools and universities should have been sufficient to meet the country's needs, if the education provided did in fact impart those skills required in a modern industrial society. But this was doubtful. The whole educational system has been vitiated by a theoretical, classical bias, copied from the French model. This has been partially remedied by the development of technical education in the 1960s. But the trouble lies deeper. In France, a theoretical classical training is in fact provided; in Turkey it is only attempted, the attempt being frustrated by a shortage of qualified teachers. So while a rapid expansion of primary education was practicable and useful, a similarly rapid expansion of university education lowered standards which were already none too high. Lectures delivered through megaphones to large concourses of students became a feature of university life in Istanbul. While such overcrowding was general, some faculties, mostly those with older traditions, managed to preserve a reasonable standard and one that was well above Middle Eastern norms. The Istanbul Faculty of Medicine, the Istanbul Technical University, the old Civil Service training school which was moved to Ankara and renamed School of Political Science, continued to provide solid training. The new Middle East Technical University in Ankara, a Westernsupported institution which uses English as its language of instruction, promised well for the future. Elsewhere the 1960s have seen a tremendous expansion of university facilities, with new universities or faculties in Erzurum in the east, Izmir in the west and Trabzon in the north. There are plans for similar facilities in Edirne, Konya and Adana. Like many more advanced countries, Turkey clearly opted for quantity before quality, a choice that may have been inevitable in view of the vocal demand for higher education by the country's youth. Demand has been consistently ahead of supply.

In 1965, for example, there were 18,000 university places for 27,000 applicants. Students in search of quality and special skills have gone abroad in ever-increasing numbers – to Germany, the United States, Britain and France. As the number of Turkish students in foreign universities increased, so did the number of those who preferred to stay abroad after graduating. There were, as a result, recurrent complaints about the number of young Turkish doctors practising in Germany and the United States.

As the pressure on the state system increased and its defects became obvious, more and more parents turned to private schools and colleges for the education of their children, a trend reinforced by the rules governing military service. Service was deferred until the completion of full-time education, and graduates of lycées and universities served as reserve officers. This created a demand for educational establishments which would keep students for as long as possible. Apart from these 'colleges of convenience', there were also a number of private institutions which did in fact provide a better education than could be found in the state system. Traditionally, most of these were wholly or partly foreign. To the extent that Turkish education had been inspired by foreign – mainly French – ideas, there was obviously an advantage in going directly to the original: in foreign schools the arts and sciences of Western civilization were taught by people born to that civilization. In addition, there were the usual advantages of a private education: smaller classes, better teachers and better facilities.

At first these foreign schools – French, Italian, German, American, English and Austrian – catered mainly for the non-Muslim subjects of the Ottoman Empire, among whom they were often accused of stirring up sedition. Later, when Muslim Turks became preponderant among students, the charge was varied. Now the schools were accused of alienating these young Turks, of bringing them up in a foreign way of life. The schools were criticized for being nationally as well as socially divisive. There was, certainly, much jealousy of the more civilized life their students led and of the much brighter prospects of private employ-ment (particularly with foreign firms and agencies) which they enjoyed. There were, therefore, constant attempts to circumscribe and even to stop altogether foreign educational enterprises, particularly as foreign schools could count on few friends among the wielders of political power, most of whom had come up a harder way. But while foreign schools and colleges – among which the American Robert College was pre-eminent – had produced few politicians and even fewer soldiers, their influence on modern Turkish literature and thought was profound and they provided a disproportionately large part of the Turkish élite.

The westernization of Turkish literature began long before the Republic was founded. In Ottoman times there had been, roughly speaking, two literatures – that of the educated classes, and folk literature. Ottoman learned literature – which was largely though not exclusively practised in Court circles – was a type of classical Islamic literature. Not only was it inspired by Persian and, to a lesser extent, Arabic models; it used as far as possible the vocabulary, the grammar, the prosody and generally the style of these original models. Official 'high Ottoman' was an artificial, but nevertheless a rich and crafts-manlike language which had only one disadvantage: it could not be understood by Arab, Persian or Turk without special training.

Folk literature, consisting of poetry, largely of dervish inspiration, romances and simple comedies (for the *Karagöz* shadow plays and other forms of popular entertainment), led a separate existence, linked with 'high literature' only by the common feeling and to some extent the common imagery of the Islamic religion. Then, in the nineteenth century, two processes developed simultaneously, the simplification of 'high Ottoman' and the imitation of Western literary models, which became more readily accessible through translations. As the press was also developing rapidly (from small beginnings in the 1830s), the typical Ottoman man of letters was a journalist-translator-creative writer. The demands of journalism led naturally to a simpler, more easily comprehensible style. The influence of Western literature operated in the same direction. The turn of the century thus saw the development of a Turkish literature – of no great originality, it is true – reasonably accessible to most literate Turks.

It was a promising beginning, but the promise of the development of a genuine national Turkish literature has remained largely unfulfilled for two main reasons. The first is the overwhelming impact of Western models, which could only be imitated, never emulated. Thus from a Turkish Corneille (who came a bit late in the day – in the nineteenth century – in the person of the poet-dramatist Abdülhak Hamit), Turkish literature has progressed through a Turkish Flaubert, a Turkish Zola, a Turkish Gorky to a Turkish Proust, a Turkish Silone, a Turkish Steinbeck, even a Turkish James Joyce and a Turkish W. H. Auden. This imitativeness still continues: just as Turkish theatre managers go to London at the beginning of each season in search of new plays to translate and produce, so Turkish publishers and translators fall over each other to present to the Turkish reader the latest Western best-seller, Nobel prize-winner or *succès d'estime*. The original is first translated, then imitated. The other reason has been the very process of simplifying the Turkish language. Again, partly under the inspiration of German and other European linguistic nationalists, a process that began as a simplification of language developed into an attempt at the 'purification' of Turkish from all Eastern (Persian and Arabic), but not Western loan words. With Mustafa Kemal Atatürk's official blessing, pure Turkish neologisms came pouring in, until official Turkish became a form of the language that was, if anything, as unintelligible to the mass of the people as 'high Ottoman' had been. Atatürk then called a halt, but in subsequent years the process of 'purification' was taken up enthusiastically by intellectuals. Their inventiveness once again outstripped popular usage and acceptance, until all contact was lost between 'progressive socialist realists' operating in Istanbul and Ankara, and the mass of readers who, by that time, had fortunately the Turkish versions of Western popular newspapers and magazines to console them. At various stages in the development of modern Turkish literature, optimists purported to see signs of a genuine synthesis between foreign elements and local traditions, and to have heard a new and genuinely Turkish creative voice. There have been Turkish writers who have been able to move their fellow-countrymen, perhaps none more effectively than the nineteenth-century patriot poet Namık Kemal (known as the 'poet of liberty'), who provided inspiration and self-justification for the Young Turkish revolutionaries of 1908.

Few literary imitations have not undergone some local change, often a change that their authors did not intend. Turkish 'socialist realist' theatrical writing of today, with its stock types of wicked landowners, down-trodden peasants and progressive intellectuals, derives more from a local tradition of popular pantomimes (called *tulûat* theatre) than from Western models. Turkey's most successful novel of recent years, Yaşar Kemal's *Ince Mehmet* (translated as *Mehmet, My Hawk*) is, for all its progressive message, a *destan*, a tale of stirring deeds by a local hero as told by generations of bazaar storytellers. Even straight journalistic reportage, like Mahmut Makal's *Bizim Köy* (translated as *A Village in Anatolia*) has overtones of the pleas for reforms with which Ottoman officials used to bombard the Court. A genre that has, however, no direct Ottoman antecedents, is the atmospheric and, generally, rather sad short story which found a master in Sait Faik – a compassionate observer of the run-down condition of interbellic Istanbul. Compassion is also the strongest feeling in the short and long-short stories of Orhan Kemal – who has produced many excellent, closely observed auto-biographic *vignettes*, but is less happy when trying to devise a fictional excuse for 'progressive' political demands. Finally, Nazım Hikmet, the Turkish Communist poet and probably the Turkish writer best-known abroad, had the personal misfortune of having suffered prolonged persecution and imprisonment for his beliefs, with the result that his progressive pleas have a power that is lacking in the writings of the arm-chair revolutionaries of Istanbul. What is more, Nazım Hikmet came to know the Turkish people in prison – and not exclusively in the person of servants, waiters and taxi-drivers, as was the case with many of his fellow writers. What he did have in common with them was a desire to refashion Turkish society from above, a desire which is the hall-mark of Turkish intellectuals.

This political preoccupation, as well as linguistic experimentation, has prevented Turkish literature from taking off beyond the surrounding peaks of Western literature. But if a genuine Turkish voice and with it works of genuine international merit are yet to be created, the swell of literary activity has increased beyond all measure. Growth of literacy and improvement in communications have for the first time created a large popular market for the written word, a demand which seeks satisfaction beyond the available media of newspapers, magazines and pulp literature.

Demand has stimulated supply in other media too, including theatre and broadcasting. Modern Turkish theatre, which owes its beginnings in the last century to the enterprise of Istanbul Armenians, and its inspiration once again to Western models, impresses the observer both by the extent of its activity and the quality of its acting and production. In Istanbul, it is not unusual to have twenty simultaneous theatrical productions. Audiences are large and interest in acting lively. In Ankara a state conservatoire, a state theatre and ballet maintain genuinely high standards. Interest in Western classical music – as well as in pop – has grown tremendously. In all these areas, Western teachers have sown in fertile ground. In theatrical production, Karl Ebert, one of the many German refugees from Nazism to whom Turkey gave employment and to whom it owes many of its cultural and academic achievements, did much to form local talent. Dame Ninette de Valois, was similarly successful in starting a ballet school in Turkey. This extensive cultural activity distinguishes Turkey from its neighbours to the east and south. Nevertheless, the country produces more talented practitioners than original creators. Turkey's educated élite has benefited from this cultural expansion, but the lower classes are still excluded, to a great degree, from its advantages.

The existence of two nations within Turkey is evident in the unequal provision of medical services. Facilities and personnel are anyway limited: in 1966 there were some 10,000 doctors (or 3·2 per 10,000 inhabitants), 60,000 hospital beds and less than 3,000 trained nurses. Although the professional qualifications of the best doctors are very good indeed, and in Istanbul and Ankara there are facilities for the most complicated forms of treatment, over large areas of the country health services are scarce. In 1962, when the first post-war Five Year Plan was being drawn up, it was calculated that there was one doctor per 635 inhabitants in Istanbul, one per 2,600 in fifteen relatively developed provinces and one per 9,400 in the remaining fifty-one provinces. Similarly, while there were more than twenty-one hospital beds per 10,000 inhabitants in the four richest provinces, there were less than five per 10,000 in fifteen provinces and less than ten per 10,000 in thirty-four provinces. Since then, the situation has been somewhat improved by the introduction of a free health service in eastern Anatolia.

Also, the number of workers benefiting from social security legislation has increased steadily: at the end of 1965 it stood at 840,000 out of an estimated total active population of 13,200,000. The Turkish pharma‑ceutical industry, which developed in a remarkably short space of time during the 1950s, not only supplies almost all the country's necessary drugs, but seems to be able to do it much more cheaply than its counterparts in the West. Important as these advances have been, the absence of proper medical services remains one of the main, if not the main complaint of the people, particularly of the rural popula‑tion. The complaint is justified. For example, Turkey's rate of infantile mortality is fantastically high: in 1960 it was estimated at 165 per thousand (United Kingdom 24 per thousand).

Once the perils of infancy have been surmounted, most Turks seem to lead a healthy and often a long life without benefit of medicine – the average life expectancy is estimated to be fifty‑five. Successful official campaigns to supply the population with preventive medicine have been one reason for this. Malaria, which a generation ago was in fact endemic over large parts of the country, has nearly disappeared. Tuberculosis has probably been brought under control. The incidence of trachoma – an eye disease at one time extremely common in eastern and southern Turkey – is decreasing rapidly. Although Turkey is by‑and‑large a poor country, nobody – or hardly anybody – starves. According to statistical data (in nutrition, unlikely to be more than the roughest approximations), in 1960 a Turk consumed on an average 2,830 calories a day (UK 3,290 calories) including 85 grammes of protein (UK 86). (The Turkish figure for 1964 was 3,110 calories – indicating an improvement either in consumption or in methods of calculation.) The usual diet of the Anatolian peasant seems adequate, if monotonous. *Bulgur pilâvı* – a pilaff made with boiled and pounded whole wheat, is the staple dish; rice is considered a luxury. Fruit and vegetables, particularly beans – are plentiful. Yoghourt finds its way into most meals – as an *hors d'oeuvre*, a pudding, a sauce or, most commonly, mixed with water and salt as a drink.

While the tremendous increase in population suggests that Turkey is becoming even healthier, urbanization poses its own problems. The shanties on the outskirts of large cities cannot be left to their own devices, as the villages have been for most of their history. Piped water, sewers and proper housing are here a much better safeguard for health than doctors and medicine. Progress has been considerable in the provision of piped water and of sewers. Although supply is constantly being overtaken by demand, Istanbul and Ankara are within sight of achieving minimum acceptable standards. Housing, on the other hand, has been badly neglected.

Until fairly recently, state activity in housing was limited to the provision of lodging quarters for civil and military officials, in provincial and other isolated postings. The right to a *lojman* (as official housing is known in Turkish bureaucratic jargon) was thus mainly a middle-class perquisite. The only exception to this was the provision of hostels for some workers in state enterprises. Housing was otherwise left in private hands and, since before the Second World War urbanization was slow, private enterprise could on the whole meet the needs of the population. After the war the stock of houses and house ownership were extended by such well-known devices as bank credits and the formation of housing cooperatives. The latter were particularly important; there was hardly an organized occupational group that did not have its own cooperative, while other cooperatives functioned as speculative ventures. Cooperatives, credits and private building of rented accommodation (which was encouraged by the gradual decontrol of rents after the war) managed to satisfy middle-class, and to a lesser extent, lower middle-class demand (while, alas, often ruining the landscape of once-beautiful cities). But the poor and peasant migrants were left to their own devices. The result was a mushrooming of squatters' shacks known in Turkish as *gecekondu* or 'put-up-in-the-night'. As Turkish law made it difficult for authorities to demolish a house with a roof on it, the *gecekondu* was often literally put up in one night before the police arrived to challenge the builders. These shacks became the focus of political and administrative controversy. Promises to legalize existing shacks, or even to issue the occupants with title-deeds, were easy ways to gain the squatters' votes. Conversely, 'strong' governors and ministers who took existing building and public health regulations seriously, organized forays into the squatters' settlements, and bulldozed their shacks to the ground. While this battle raged over the legality of the shacks, and while governments (particularly that of Adnan Menderes) were accused of violating building regulations for fear of offending the electorate, little effort was made to provide alterna-tive accommodation. Only in the middle 1960s were the first plans drawn up to build cheap municipal houses and to defer the demolition of shacks until these houses became available. But with some two and a half million people living in urban shacks in the middle 1960s, the size of the problem was such that it would clearly be years before it could be solved. Equally clearly, not only official help, but self-help would have to be mobilized.

At the time of the 1965 census, of the 5·5 million households in Turkey, 4·6 million paid no rent. The majority of these were peasant families, the number of middle-class families owning their own houses being very small. The number of families paying monthly rents in excess of TL400 ($44 at the official rate of exchange) was only 41,000. These figures show not only how small the Turkish middle class is but also the extent to which Turkey is still outside a money economy. The same conclusions are suggested by employment statistics: of 13 million people of working age in Turkey in 1965, 9·4 million people were employed in agriculture, the total number of people receiving wages and salaries being 2·4 million. However, rates of change are important here too. The number of people employed in industry rose by ten per cent between 1960 and 1965, while the number of wage and salary earners increased by twenty-five per cent. Nevertheless, subsistence agriculture, self-help and generally taking in each other's washing, without any money changing hands, is still a feature of Turkish society. This is reflected in the smallness of the gross national product per person expressed in money terms: $275 per person per year in 1966 (United Kingdom $1,810 in 1965; Greece $590 in 1964). While this figure gives some idea of Turkey's comparative poverty, comparison with other countries is made difficult because so much in Turkish life cannot be reflected in calculations of national product, however sophisticated one's system of 'weighting' the figures. To give a simple example, the provision of piped water shows up in national product figures, while the money value of a well in a peasant's back yard is difficult to calculate. Conversely, the current increase in the value of the national product –

an increase which will almost certainly be rapid in the next few years – is partly attributable to urbanization and industrialization and only partly to an authentic improvement in the standard of living.

Scarcity of money and dependence on natural phenomena and other acts of God are reflected in the habits, values and ideals of Turkish society. These habits and values have, of course, been moulded in the first place by Islam, as well as by the peculiar social structure of the Turks throughout the ages, by the fact, that is, that they were a nation of peasants, soldiers and administrators. To such people a cavalier treatment of money came naturally. Money was to be spent and enjoyed, when available, and if earned, earned quickly, as by a soldier coming home loaded with booty. 'Hitting money' (*para vurmak*), like hitting and capturing an enemy, is still the ideal of a Turk in the novel and uncongenial field of business. Thrift is as new a virtue as banking is a new institution, and every Turkish bank has to run a constant lottery for account holders in order to attract customers. With this attitude towards money came military and peasant virtues – courage, generosity and hospitality and a conception of honour, or 'face' which it is extremely easy to affront, indeed, which watches for affronts. To mitigate the uncertainties of life and of nature, the Turks had developed, in addition to a limited soldierly (but not commercial) form of self-help, a habit of mutual help that, in the great period of the Ottoman Empire in the sixteenth century, was the envy of European travellers. This derived largely from Islamic law, in which alms-giving is one of the five main duties of the faithful. The provision of mosques, schools, inns, fountains, bath-houses, the distribution of food to the poor, particularly on religious holidays, were the usual ways in which the rich and powerful acquired merit. Secularization has reduced the scope, but not yet entirely eliminated this form of social assistance. In the 1950s when traditional social habits reasserted themselves under the Menderes administration, private associations for the building of mosques sprang up in many places.

Personal and mutual assistance has continued in some old forms and in at least one new form. The basic unit of mutual help is, of course, the extended family. The obligation to help needy members of a family, particularly the old and the young, is absolute. Households remain large, with a national average of five to seven persons per house-hold in 1965, when nearly two million households had seven or more members. The ties of locality and neighbourhood are important, particularly, of course, in villages, which in law and usually in fact, are corporate bodies. Villages can own land in common and, incidentally, are often in conflict with other corporate bodies, that is, surrounding villages, over land rights. Professional guilds and corporations have almost disappeared, except perhaps in the case of the officer corps, which, while often riven by internal dissensions, resents outside civilian interference. Protocol, which requires the local commanding officer to congratulate the senior administrator on 29 October – the anniversary of the proclamation of the Republic – and the latter to return the compliment in person on 30 August – the anniversary of the defeat of the Greeks in the Turkish War of Independence – is one small instance of the separate existence of the military institution.

Networks of mutual help and patronage are perhaps most evident in the two main political parties, which in the middle 1960s were the Republican People's Party and the Justice Party. As we have seen, the first was largely a mutual aid society for the educated, the second for the rest of the population. The parties subsume local groups, clans, friendships and interests in genuine groupings that re-create themselves as soon as and as often as they are closed down by authority. These parties are thus much more authentic associations than any that might be based solely on political principles. Even ostensibly ideological associations can sometimes be explained in terms of kinship or another social relationship. Relationships in general are seldom anonymous (as in the industrial West). Business, official or private, is based usually on personal contacts. The visiting-cards of rich and influential people circulate throughout society, smoothing the paths of their less fortunate brethren. The taxi-driver who addresses his customer as 'Elder Brother' is, as a Turkish sociologist has pointed out to me, using a colloquialism which reflects a tradition of personal, as distinct from official, deference and, therefore, implies a claim for personal consideration. Whatever the law may say, a good man is one who helps his family, friends, and anyone who has a valid albeit importunate claim on his interest and protection. The asperities of a French-type bureaucracy are thus tamed and civilized. Throughout the country backing (*arka*, literally 'back') is all-important.

But not everyone benefits from this subtle network of protection. Furthermore, traditional forms of paternalism are decreasing and are almost wholly absent from certain fields of activity. The private industrialist, or for that matter the state as an industrial employer does not, unlike his Japanese counterpart, accept responsibility for the welfare of his employees. Industries with seasonal patterns of employ-ment lay off work-people with complete unconcern for their future livelihood. This may be perhaps because industry and trade are new activities which have not been permeated, as the Civil Service had been, with the tradition that 'God will not prosper a man who deprives one of His servants of the divinely appointed means of livelihood (*rızkullah*)', a tradition which has often fortunately mitigated administrative cuts and reorganization. However that may be, trade unions, when they began to be formed in earnest after the Second World War, had an important job to do, and the right to strike, which was formally granted in 1963, was a valuable weapon.

The undeniable existence of social injustice and inequality – particularly in new fields of activity and modern surroundings – has led many Turks to sneer at the old Republican slogan, 'We are a nation welded together without classes and privileges.' This claim, which was in fact a restatement of the old concept of the brotherhood of Islam, is not entirely void of meaning. The Turkish nation had been, as we have seen, welded by Islam and by the united hostility of its Christian neighbours, into a close offensive-defensive formation – which forty-five years of peace (probably the longest uninterrupted spell of peace the Turks have known) have not yet broken up. This sense of unity can be a diminishing asset, but it is still an asset tending to mitigate, even where it cannot avoid, civil discord. Divided as the Turks often are today by culture, way of life, education, material and social advantages, and, increasingly, by political beliefs, the tradition of Islamic frontiersmen who had to stand together lest they fell separately, still makes a greater degree of internal cohesion in Turkey than can be seen in many neighbouring countries. Istanbul University students who, in April 1960, marched against armed policemen, chanting the lament of Gazi Osman Pasha, the defender of Plevna against the Russians in 1877, with its refrain 'Can such a thing happen? Can brother strike brother?' were appealing to a sentiment still alive. It is the same sentiment which has so far blocked the path to extremists in Turkish politics.

The Republic has brought many new holidays to the Turkish calendar, but it has not suppressed the old religious ones, which are in fact the ones felt to be real, rather than official holidays. The two main Muslim festivals (*bayram*) are the *Şeker Bayramı* (Sugar Festival), celebrated at the end of the Ramadan (Ramazan in Turkish) and the *Kurban Bayramı* (Festival of the Sacrifices) which marks the season of the pilgrimage to Mecca. Both are treated as public holidays and last three to four days, when all offices are closed. They are also marked by the usual holiday features: new clothes, gifts, fun fairs, visits to the eldest member of the family (whose hand is ceremoniously kissed) and so forth. They are fixed in the Muslim lunar calendar, which means that they move round the solar year. Other Muslim holy days – the Prophet's Birthday, the commemoration of the revelation of the Koran, etc., are observed by religious people, but are not treated as public holidays. Official republican holidays are Republic Day (or rather two and a half days, starting on 29 October), National Sovereignty Day (23 April, the anniversary of the opening of the first Grand National Assembly in Ankara), 1 May (called Spring Day rather than Labour Day, although traditionally the Spring festival was celebrated on *Hidrellez*, that is, St George's Day, 23 April in the Julian and, therefore, 6 May in the Gregorian Calendar), Youth Day (19 May – the anniversary of Mustafa Kemal's landing at Samsun at the start of his campaign in Anatolia), Freedom Day (27 May – the anniversary of the 1960 coup) and Victory Day (30 August). This adds up to a considerable number of days on which no business can be transacted (although it is an improvement on the state of affairs in Ottoman Istanbul when Friday, the Muslim day of rest, the Jewish Sabbath and Christian Sunday were all equally barren of business). In addition, the anniversary of the death of Atatürk on 10 November is marked as a day of mourning when places of entertainment are closed, no alcoholic drink may be served in restaurants, but more serious business goes on. Most cities also have

Liberation Days to mark the withdrawal of Greek, French, British or other foreign troops after the First World War. Finally, there are official holidays that did not quite come off, like National Coastal Shipping Day on 1 July. Cities have now got used to the Continental (but emphatically not to the English) week-end. In the villages Friday – the day of community prayers – is still the unofficial day of rest.

In the tenor of people's private lives, there is again a dichotomy between the small urban élite and the more or less traditional groups. At one extreme, the customs and habits of the international bourgeoisie are faithfully reproduced. Like their secularized counterparts in the West, the Turkish middle class marries in register offices without benefit of religion, has few children, divorces expeditiously, and has a quick brush with religion following death, for even modern families will have a *mevlid* (a poem celebrating the birth of the Prophet, which is traditionally recited as a requiem) said for the repose of the soul of a dead relative. At the other extreme, even the legal requirement of a registry marriage is dispensed with, and traditional ceremonies mark the great occasions of life: circumcision (performed usually when the boy is seven years old), marriage and death. In the villages and small market towns, marriages are usually arranged and bride price paid or the bride is captured ('taken to the mountains', willingly or unwillingly), when a vendetta usually follows. Expensive rejoicings (*düğün*) are organized to celebrate a circumcision or marriage. It is a traditional act of piety to pay for circumcision parties of indigent boys, and in towns, group circumcisions are often organized and followed by large-scale popular entertainment with music, song and puppets, clowns, acrobats and magicians (while the élite, who also have their boys circumcised, send them without any fuss to the nearest hospital or private clinic).

Not everyone can afford an expensive circumcision party, but a wedding is usually celebrated in great style, except by the poorest. In more developed areas, such as western Anatolia, the procession when the bride is taken to the bridegroom's house, has been usually replaced by a motorcade of taxis, jeeps, buses and even tractors, with the bride still usually veiled at least for this one day. Funerals, in true Islamic style are simple and are attended only by men. They take place (or, in the phrase which gives an idea of the matter-of-factness of the occasion, 'the body is lifted') usually within twenty-four hours of death. Cemeteries, which in Istanbul and other cities were one of the most graceful features of the urban scene – with upright headstones, surmounted by turbans signifying the rank of the dead man, become progressively simpler as one moves into the country, until in some villages they are little more than fields planted with slabs of rock. In towns, as in villages, the graves of holy men (*türbe*, or in pure Turkish *yatır*) are held in honour, and in spite of official prohibition, visited by the faithful or the superstitious. Here animals are often sacrificed in thanksgiving, or as a request for intercession. In the countryside, even more primitive forms of superstition survive and one often comes across trees festooned with petitioners' strips of clothing. Miraculous wells and springs abound, usually having been inherited by the Turks from their Christian predecessors. The wearing of amulets – blue beads to ward off the evil eye, passages from the Koran or prayers written on scraps of paper which are then folded and sewn in a triangular bag (*muska*), is extremely common.

Superstition is more widespread among women for obvious educational, social and psychological reasons. However, it is dangerous to generalize about the lives of women in Turkey. Turkish society is moving, in a sense, from differentiation to uniformity, and of all the forms of differentiation perhaps none was stronger than that between the sexes. The state of women in traditional Turkish Muslim society is usually described as one of complete subjection to men. There is, of course, much truth in this view, although women like other social groups had their rights – rights under the marriage contract, which usually included a settlement on the wife, rights of inheritance (a daughter's share being half that of a son), and so forth. Moreover, from the city harem, women's apartments or the peasant's cottage, women often exercised considerable influence on men's private and public conduct. Veiling and seclusion were always an urban phenomenon, inapplicable to villages where women did much of the field work. Today formal equality is qualified by the survival of traditional attitudes, as well as by lack of opportunities. Although there are many women teachers, secretaries, junior civil servants as well as highly publicized women judges, lawyers and doctors, Turkey remains largely

133

a masculine society which looks askance at unaccompanied and un-attached women. Excepting the urban élite, mixed parties are still a new, limited and slightly uncomfortable experience. In Anatolia the absence of women from coffee houses and eating places is almost total. The equally marked absence of waitresses and manageresses contributes to a barrack-room atmosphere of rough-and-ready untidiness which has struck so many perceptive travellers. Fathers, elder brothers, husbands and elder sons have the role of protecting and ruling over their womenfolk. It is a role which, particularly in the cities, is becoming more and more difficult to play, and with the growth of primary education in mixed schools, leading to an increasing number of girls going on to secondary and higher education, traditional values will have to be adjusted not only to new laws but, more important, to new social realities. At present there are many cases of maladjustment – among the élite divorce is common, while throughout society tension between the sexes often erupts in crime, although in the absence of reliable statistics, it is difficult to say whether sexual offences have increased as much as a casual reading of Turkish newspapers would suggest.

Throughout Turkey groups and group codes are breaking down. Ottoman society was a mosaic of clearly defined groups: Muslim and non-Muslim, natives and foreigners, speakers of different languages, inhabitants of different places, the learned and the ignorant, members of different trades, soldiers, administrators and peasants, men and women – all had different roles and different customs. The multiplicity of local groups made it easier for Turks to accept the foreigner as somebody whose customs had to be respected. Even now a foreigner will find it easiest at times to explain refusing a service or an invitation by saying 'This is not customary in my country'. Differences in customs were, and to a large extent still are, taken for granted by a differentiated society. But as the country moves from a concept of group-membership to one of uniform citizenship tolerance, paradoxically, tends to decrease, particularly as group ethics are now officially based on nationalism. True, in Atatürk's conception, nationalism is supplemented by the idea of civilization as a universal code of (material and, perhaps, human) values. But nationalism and civilization are less imperative determinants

134

of personal behaviour than the old religious and social values, whose large-scale, albeit precarious, survival gives Turkey its distinctive features and, as some would have it, its distinctive virtues. In the meantime the fact that the crust of uniform, official westernization has been broken by the emergence of a large, increasingly powerful and semi-traditional lower-middle class should not obscure the direction of change towards a Western-type technological society. But that goal is still some way off, and may itself change before it is reached.

9   The country

AS LONG AS THE PRESENT RATE of development continues, any description of the Turkish scene is bound to be overtaken by events and made obsolete almost before the ink is dry. This rapid change is not limited to the social scene. Even the geography of the country is changing. Tourists going today to Antalya or to neighbouring resorts along the Turkish Mediterranean coast (known as the 'Turkish Riviera' in travel agents' literature) are unlikely to recognize the follow-ing description of the region published as recently as 1946:

> In spite of the fertility of the plain of Antalya, the density of population is the same as in the steppes of Central Anatolia. The reason lies in the extremely unhealthy climatic conditions. In the summer the plain of Antalya is unbearably hot; malaria rages wherever there is as much as a puddle of stagnant water. The sparse population of the plain spends the summer in the mountains. In this season the Antalya plain, with its antique ruins, lies deserted under the burning sun, resembling a wonderful necropolis, a city of the dead.[27]

It is, of course, still hot in Antalya in the summer, but tourists do not find it unbearable – they seem to revel in it. Malaria has been eliminated from the region, as it has been from almost the whole of Turkey. The population, which has been increasing steadily, cannot all leave in the summer: the tourists have to be looked after, a local textile factory has to be manned. What has happened is that this part of Turkey – the antique Pamphylia – is enjoying almost its first period of prosperity since late Roman times. A similar transformation has taken place – in most cases since the last war – in many other parts of Turkey. Thus we read in a recent archaeological guide to Aegean Turkey:

> Great changes have taken place in the Maeander valley during the last few years. Whereas formerly the river used to flood the plain every winter, and Miletus was approached by a rough track ... now a large part of the plain has been reclaimed, a fine new road has been driven across from Söke to Milâs, and cars may reach Miletus all the year round.[28]

And great as the changes have been here – with the Söke plain trans-formed from a marsh into one of the richest cotton-growing areas of Turkey, they are only a beginning. Under a Great Maeander (Büyük Menderes in Turkish) Valley Plan announced in 1967, $300 million are to be invested to irrigate another 260,000 hectares of land.

However, not all the changes have been for the better. Even before the war it was noticed that areas marked green on official Turkish maps had been denuded of forests. The destruction of forests has been particularly rapid in the 1940s and 1950s – since when draconian measures have stabilized and, probably, started to improve the situation. In the meantime, the destruction of forests has increased the ravages of erosion. A German geographer[29] who studied the effects of a rain storm near Ankara in 1933 calculated that during it, every hectare of affected land had lost thirty-four tons of topsoil. The Soviet geographer Matveyev wrote in 1946: 'The struggle against erosion in Anatolia presents a problem which will undoubtedly grow in acuteness with the extension and intensification of agriculture.' Since then the cultivated area has been almost doubled – from thirteen to twenty-five million hectares – and large parts of central Turkey have predictably become a dust-bowl.

These changes have, of course, to be seen in the context of the permanent features of Turkish geography. Here, one is again immediately struck by tremendous contrasts, for just as there are two nations in Turkey, so there are, in a way, two countries – the Turkey of the coasts, with its Mediterranean and, at times, sub-tropical climate; and the uplands, a land of wide vistas of almost central Asian severity.

The area of Turkey is 301 thousand square miles (781 thousand square km.) or more than three times that of the United Kingdom. All but nine thousand square miles of it lie in Asia. In the rectangle that is Asia Minor, or Anatolia, the mountains run roughly from east to west, radiating from a high mountainous region on the confines of the Soviet Union, Persia and Iraq. Here, high volcanic peaks rise above the plateau that used to bear the name of Armenia. Today Mount Ararat (Ağrı Dağ in Turkish, 5,165 metres high) lies on the Turkish side of the frontier with Soviet Armenia. A little to the south, Little Ararat rises to a height of 3,915 metres, while to the southeast, on the north shore of Lake Van (known to local inhabitants as the Sea of Van because of its size which extends to 3,700 square kilometres), Mount Süphan Dağ reaches a height of 4,170 metres. South of the lake, Cilo Dağ (4,170 metres) overlooks the wild Kurdish country, lying north of the frontier with Iraq. Cilo Dağ is situated in the extreme south-eastern province of Hakkâri, once inhabited by the Assyrians – Nestorian Christians of Mesopotamian origin who were driven out of their mountain villages in the First World War, when they were unwise enough to side with the Russians. They have been replaced largely by their neighbours and enemies, the nomadic Kurds, who have neglected the cultivated terraces cut by the Assyrians into the steep valley slopes, so that the whole region has become half-deserted and derelict. Yet even this remote area, where few foreigners could and few Turks bothered to penetrate until the late 1950s, is being opened up. It is skirted by the new CENTO road from Iskenderun on the Mediterranean to Rezaiyeh in Persia. By 1967 this road had reached Cizre in the west and the Persian frontier in the east. Cilo Dağ itself has been visited, amongst others, by British schoolboy explorers and adventurous Embassy secretaries from Ankara.

The eastern Anatolian mountains form a watershed between the Black Sea and the Caspian to the east, and the Black Sea and the Persian Gulf to the south. One of the rivers which has its source in the region is the Aras (Araxes) which flows into the Caspian. On one of its tributaries, the frontier stream of Arpaçay, the Turks and the Russians agreed in 1966 to build a large dam. Further west lie the headwaters of the Tigris (Dicle in Turkish), the Euphrates (Fırat) and of their many tributaries. One of the tributaries of the Tigris is the Batman Suyu which gives its name to Turkey's main oilfield. Since January 1967 this oilfield has been linked by a 500-kilometre pipeline to Dörtyol on the Gulf of Iskenderun. This eighteen inch pipeline which has an annual capacity of over 3·5 million tons of oil, was built in almost exactly one year, raising in Turkish minds the hope that similar lines would be constructed through Turkish territory to connect with Persian oilfields in the east and Iraqi ones in the southeast. The first step was taken in this direction in 1967 when Turkish and Iraqi experts started to study a project for a natural gas pipeline from Kirkuk to Iskenderun. The development of these schemes would, of course, revolutionize the economy of eastern Turkey. The same is true of the giant dam at Keban on the Euphrates, work on which began in 1966 and which is due for completion in 1971. The cost of the Keban dam scheme has been estimated at some $300 million. The dam is to produce six billion kW/hr. of electricity a year and irrigate a vast area. Another project which will bring benefit to eastern Turkey is the linking of the Turkish and Persian railway networks which is being financed by the Central Treaty Organization. In 1964 the Turkish eastern railhead was extended to Tatvan on the shores of Lake Van. When this scheme is completed there will be three railway lines linking Turkey with its eastern neighbours, the other two being the link with the Soviet Union through Erzurum and Kars in the north, and the old Baghdad Railway in the south.

In social welfare the province of Muš, lying to the west of Lake Van, was selected for the first experiment in providing a free comprehensive health service, which has now been extended to the surrounding provinces.

Erzurum, the chief city of eastern Turkey, is the seat of the Atatürk University which was planned specifically as a regional university and was given the task of raising local standards in agriculture and animal husbandry.

However, this enumeration of recent projects and advances should not blind us to the fact that eastern Anatolia, which is essentially a poor area, relying for its livelihood on unscientific agriculture and cattle-breeding, is overstocked, overgrazed and underdeveloped. Brigandage, although now no longer an everyday occurrence, has still not been stamped out. The Kurds, who form a large part of the local population, are not yet fully settled, or assimilated. While the whole area is nominally under civilian rule, which after the last war was extended even to the wild mountain country of Dersim (province of Tunçeli, southwest of Erzurum), the power of the army is often paramount. Erzurum, until recently the headquarters of the Third Land Army, is primarily a vast cantonment. In the south, there is a large air base at Diyarbakır. Eastern Anatolia is traditionally an unruly frontier country (*serhat* in Turkish), where the arts of peace are being learned slowly, and the fruits of peace are only just beginning to come in.

From the Black Sea, eastern Turkey is separated by the eastern and highest part of the North Anatolian range (known also as the Pontic Alps). This range, or rather series of parallel ranges, divided by narrow valleys, stretches along the whole length of the Black Sea coast and has an extension in the Istranca mountains in Turkish Thrace. At its eastern end, the North Anatolian mountains reach a height of over 3,900 metres (Kaçkar Dağ, 3,937 metres), sinking gradually as one travels west along the coast. A number of fast-flowing rivers rise in the inner ranges, flow for a time in the valleys between the ranges, roughly parallel to the coast, until they find a weak spot in the coastal barrier through which they work their way into the Black Sea. From east to west the main rivers are the Çoruh, whose estuary is in Soviet territory near Batum; the Yeşilırmak (or Green River) – 400 kilometres long, on which a hydro-electric station was built in 1966 at Almus near Amasya; the Kızılırmak (Red River) – the classical Halys (950 kilometres long) with a large dam and a hydro-electric station at Hirfanli, east of Ankara, and finally the Sakarya (600 kilometres long) with a large dam at Sarıyar, and one, started in 1967, at Gökçekaya on its tributary, the river Porsuk.

To the south of the North Anatolian mountains lies the Central Anatolian plateau, to the north the Black Sea coastal plain, narrow in places and widening near the river estuaries. The seaward slopes of the mountains are covered with dense forests; the coastal strip itself is one of the most fertile and, certainly, the wettest part of Turkey. In the east, the sheltered sub-tropical coastal plain round Rize, produces enough tea to meet local demands, leaving an exportable surplus. Further west, Giresun is famous for its hazelnuts, of which Turkey is a major world producer. High-quality tobacco is grown near Samsun and Bafra. Elsewhere flax, maize and rice are grown on a fairly large scale. This concentration on cash crops, the problem of a fairly high density of population and an almost complete absence of industry, have led to a comparatively high rate of emigration, and, in bad years, to occasional malnutrition among the local inhabitants. The Black Sea coast exports, naturally enough, sailors and also cooks and bakers to the main cities and, in the old days, as far afield as Moscow. Lazes, as the inhabitants of the eastern Black Sea coast are called, whether they speak the Laz tongue (which is akin to Georgian) or not, are still the backbone of the Turkish navy and merchant marine. In popular estimation they are brave, gay, jealous, quick-tempered and enterprising – qualities which correspond roughly to the national archetype of the Georgians across the Soviet frontier. At the western end of the coast there is now a growing industrial area centred on Turkey's only important coalfield at Zonguldak (which alone meets local demand). In 1965 a large iron and steel mill was built – with American aid – at the western end of this coalfield, at Ereğli. Zonguldak has had a proper harbour since the 1950s and Samsun and Trabzon since the 1960s. Otherwise, the Black Sea coast, which is almost free of indentations and thus lacks natural harbours, is served only by open roadsteads from which passengers and cargo have to be transferred by launch or lighter. Skill in handling these frail craft in bad weather is supposed to be the distinguishing mark of the Laz sailor. Trabzon, traditionally the chief city of the coast, now has its own university, specializing in civil engineering. However, as was the case with other institutions of higher learning, this was set up before enough academic staff could be recruited. In 1967 the existence of classrooms full of students, but with no lecturers to teach them, was advertised by a series of student strikes and marches.

Like the Black Sea coast, the Mediterranean coast is cut off from the interior by a high mountain range – the Taurus. The Taurus mountains are higher and narrower than the North Anatolian range. There are several peaks rising above a height of 3,000 metres (Toros Dağı 3,585

141

metres; Aladağ 3,910 metres). In the extreme southwestern corner of Turkey the mountains, which are known here as the Western or Lycian Taurus, extend as far as the sea, leaving room only for a number of isolated and extremely picturesque valleys and bays – at Marmaris, Fethiye, Kaş, Finike, etc. This is perhaps the most beautiful part of the Turkish coast and one likely in time to attract most tourists – whose numbers will certainly increase when a coastal road is built round this very difficult mountain country. For the moment, however, the Lycian coast has to rely on the dying trade in sponges (which were marketed through Greece – an arrangement interrupted by tension over Cyprus), or horticulture (Finike oranges being particularly well-known in Turkey), and, round Fethiye, on the mining of chrome ore of which Turkey is a major world supplier, along with Rhodesia and the Soviet Union.

Further east, the Taurus turns inland leaving room for the fertile plain of Pamphylia round the port of Antalya. This, as we have seen, has only recently been freed from the scourge of malaria to become one of Turkey's most promising regions – and one selected for a regional development plan sponsored by the Food and Agriculture Organization of the United Nations. Tourism, agriculture and horticulture and a modest degree of industrialization, have already raised living standards. Communications have improved – there is a good coastal road to Alanya in the east, which will soon be extended as far as Mersin, and an inland one over the mountains to the north, while Antalya itself has a small airfield. With better road communications, out-of-season fruit and vegetables grown round Antalya can now reach markets in Istanbul and Ankara. In 1967 a hydro-electric station was built on the river Aksu, east of Antalya.

East of Antalya, the Taurus once again closes in on the sea, separating the plain of Pamphylia from the much larger Cilician plain (in Turkish, Çukurova). Here drainage and soil improvement started by the Ottoman government in the late nineteenth century, have recently been applied on a much larger scale with flood control, irrigation and hydro-electric schemes centred on the two main rivers – Seyhan and Ceyhan. The Seyhan River Plan alone provides for the drainage and irrigation of 183,000 hectares of land at an estimated cost of $250 million.

By the end of 1966 60,000 hectares had already benefited from land improvement work.

Cilicia is the main cotton-producing region of Turkey, and since cotton has displaced tobacco as Turkey's main export crop, Cilicia has grown rich. Its chief city, Adana, developed in the 1950s into a boom town by Turkish standards – with Adana millionaires becoming familiar figures, in fact as well as in fiction. Agricultural development has been supplemented by industry – there are textile mills, plants for the extraction of vegetable oil, and a large refinery at Mersin, a town which serves as the port of Adana. Social development has been uneven: the production of cash crops and the growth of associated industries has brought in poor seasonal labourers from the barren mountain regions to the north. These have joined local agricultural labourers – typically called fellahs and often Arabic-speaking, in forming a depressed proletariat. Turkoman and Kurdish tribes, settled two or three generations ago, have not yet shed all their resentment at the forcible change in their way of life, or emerged from the poverty in which they soon found themselves. In 1957, over forty per cent of the population of Adana lived in shanties. In these conditions, with national tension often underlying social tension in a pattern reminiscent of the Arab Middle East, it is not surprising that this southeastern corner of Turkey should have become a focus of left-wing agitators. In the 1960s the Adana regional office of the Turkish Confederation of Trade Unions (Türkiş) was the only one dominated by Marxists. Their influence was felt also in strikes in the Mersin and Batman oil refineries and among workers engaged in the construction of the Batman–Iskenderun pipeline.

The remaining provinces of southeastern Turkey – the province of Hatay (known as the Sandjak of Alexandretta when it was part of French-mandated Syria), and those of Gaziantep, Urfa and Mardin – are geographically, climatically, and sometimes socially and nationally a bridge area leading to the Arab lands. In Ottoman times much of this area was administered from centres – such as Aleppo and Mosul – which lie today in Arab territory. The proportion of Arabs among the local population is difficult to determine. It also varies from area to area – high in Hatay, very low in and around Gaziantep, etc. Iskenderun

(Alexandretta) is being developed as a major port, coming fourth in importance after Istanbul, Izmir and Mersin. The development started for strategic reasons in the Second World War when a British company was given the task of building installations which could handle the flow of arms and equipment necessary to protect Turkey from a German attack. Work was accelerated in the Cold War, since Iskenderun was selected as the port of supply for the Turkish Third Army in Erzurum. More recently the pipeline to Batman and the CENTO road to Persia have enhanced the importance of Iskenderun as an outlet for Near Eastern trade.

The western coasts of Turkey differ considerably from the northern and southern coastlands. Since the general direction of the mountains is east to west, western Turkey is divided laterally into large slices extending from the sea into the interior. Thanks to the river valleys which lie between the mountain ranges, communications with the interior are much easier than they are from the Black Sea or Mediterranean coasts. The valleys themselves are wider and lead to extensive fertile plains near the coast. The plains south of the Sea of Marmora and east of the Aegean – the Bithynian plain north of Bursa and the Ionian countryside round Izmir (to use the classical geographical names) – form some of the richest and most developed parts of Turkey. River control, drainage, irrigation, the mechanization of agriculture, and, above all, a spectacular improvement in communications, are everywhere raising standards. Since the expulsion of the Greeks after the First World War, this has been a land without national problems. For a while it was also a land without trade and industry. But, starting in the 1930s, industry has been developed and agriculture modernized. Izmir, the chief city of Aegean Turkey, is a flourishing commercial centre and a busy port handling the bulk of Turkey's agricultural exports. The country round Izmir produces olives, tobacco, cotton, grapes and figs – all staple constituents of Turkish exports. In the late 1930s an annual International Trade Fair was instituted, held in the second half of August and the first half of September, attracting to Izmir a considerable part of the import trade. A new development has been the growth of assembly facilities for imported foreign vehicles and other manufactured goods. Apart from industry based on local agricultural products (olive pressing, wine-making, soap-making, etc.), there are several textile mills (with carpet-making concentrated in the more traditionally Turkish areas further inland – Gördes, Uşak, Isparta, etc.). An oil refinery, the country's third, was started in Izmir in 1967. Electricity comes mainly from the Gediz dam, inaugurated by Mr Menderes shortly before he was overthrown by the army in 1960. Minerals are found on the edges of the region – boracite (known as pandermite after the port of Bandirma on the Sea of Marmora) in the north, chrome in the south, and uranium in the east.

But perhaps the richest potential of western Turkey is in tourism. Here lie the ruins of some of the most famous cities of antiquity: Troy, Pergamum, Sardis, Ephesus, Miletus, Halicarnassus and many others. With new excavation, preservation and restoration, the material environment within which our Western civilization first took shape is becoming clearly visible. There are in western Turkey more Greek antiquities than in Greece, nearly as many Roman antiquities as in Italy. Now that roads have been built and the country opened up, the ruins of antiquity can be seen with the minimum of trouble and the maximum of pleasure – ruins lying in magnificent scenery, in a generous and smiling countryside. That mass tourism started only in the middle 1960s can only be explained by the shortage of commercial skills among the Turks, but having started, world politics permitting, it is bound to grow at a tremendous rate. Western Turkey seems to be on the eve of one of its periodic ages of prosperity. It had been prosperous in classical Greek, Hellenistic, Roman, Seljuk and finally Ottoman times. The last period of prosperity before the First World War was, however, due largely to foreign enterprise and benefited above all the Greeks, who have since left. Today's prosperity can be more solidly based on indigenous effort and achievement.

Izmir has also developed once again a cultural life that is lively by Turkish standards. It has its own university, theatres and broadcasting station. It has a tradition of communicating with the West directly and not by way of Istanbul (and later Ankara), a tradition that republican centralization and Greek-Turkish hostility have circumscribed in recent years, but which will stand the city and the whole of western Turkey in good stead when the barrier between Greece and Turkey is removed and the unnatural division of the Aegean basin is ended. Already economic development no less than the settlement here of Turks expelled from the Balkans, justifies the adjective European being applied to Aegean Turkey.

European Turkey, properly speaking, is a triangle of some 9,000 square miles (24,000 square kilometres) with its apex in Istanbul at its eastern end, and bounded by the Black Sea in the north, the Sea of Marmora in the south, and the frontier with Greece and Bulgaria in the west. The wooded Istranca mountains, which are actually a continuation of the Northern Anatolian range, run roughly parallel to the Black Sea coast. The frontier with Greece follows the river Meriç (Maritza). On its banks, roughly at the point where Greece, Bulgaria and Turkey meet, lies the city of Edirne (Adrianople) which was the capital of the Ottoman sultans after Bursa and before the fall of Constantinople, and was thereafter a favourite royal residence during the hunting season. Little is left of the city's old splendour and importance except for the collection of magnificent mosques, the oldest going back to the end of the fourteenth century, while the largest and most famous is the sixteenth century mosque of Sultan Selim, built by the great Turkish architect Sinan in a spirit of obvious emulation of Santa Sophia in Istanbul. Edirne, which derived its importance from the fact that it was the first staging post to the west of Istanbul, through which the produce of the South Balkans was channelled to the Ottoman capital or straight to Europe, was devastated in the wars first with the Russians and then the Bulgarians. The decline of Edirne continued even under the Republic until after World War Two. One reason was that it had been deprived of its hinterland, another that it had lost its non-Turkish inhabitants, for by an accident of history, eastern (i.e. Turkish) Thrace had a large proportion of Greek and Bulgarian inhabitants, while western Thrace was almost purely Turkish in population when it was ceded to Greece in 1918. Today tourist motor traffic has come to the rescue of Edirne, while plans are afoot to revive its ancient tradition of learning by founding in it a new university. The rest of Thrace, west of Istanbul, is a fairly rich agricultural country producing cereals and grapes, from which high quality wines are made for the home and foreign markets.

Istanbul itself straddles Europe and Asia, being built on both sides of the Straits of Bosporus and of the Sea of Marmora, with its main centre on the European shore. Although often described as a city wholly untypical of Turkey, it is the country's head if not its heart, being the centre of commerce, industry and culture. With a population of some two million, it is the largest city in Turkey. About three-quarters of Turkish industry are concentrated in its neighbourhood – in Europe along the Orient railway, and across the Straits again along the main railway line up to and beyond Izmit (Nicomedeia). It has a large university (which like every other institution in the city is bursting at the seams), a technical university, the American Robert College (a university in all but name), and the best schools in the country. All the national newspapers and magazines are published in Istanbul. It has more and better theatres than the capital, Ankara, which however (thanks to official sponsorship) is better off in opera, ballet and music. Istanbul is today predominantly Turkish in language and population. The once numerous Greek, Armenian, Jewish and foreign trading communities number between them not much more than one tenth of the total population. In aspect, dominated as it is, and has been for centuries, by the sultans' great mosques (to which Santa Sophia has been assimilated by the addition of minarets), by the old seraglio, by the two Ottoman castles on the Bosporus and by the sultans' later baroque palaces, it looks Turkish, imperial and metropolitan. Byzantium, of course, is there too, obviously as in Santa Sophia and the Great Land Walls, and discreetly in the smaller churches; and European influences are everywhere – in the nineteenth-century slums of the old European quarter of Beyoğlu (formerly Pera), as well as in the villas of the Princes Islands. Today, of course, the predominant form of building is the block of flats. Blocks of various sizes have filled almost all the available space within the old walled city and spread well beyond it. And, of course, as in other Turkish cities, there are tens of thousands of people, mainly peasant migrants, living in shanty towns. However, the landscape, with its huge natural harbour, steep slopes leading to the sea, bays, promontories and islands can bear with almost any amount of ugliness – whether of ill-designed office blocks or of mushrooming shanties. And amongst man-made features the mosques pull together

147

a mass of indifferent building – giving shape and meaning to one of the world's greatest panoramas.

Istanbul has often been accused of having enervated the Spartan Turks, of having corrupted the purity of Islam, or alternatively of having grown superstition, reaction and intrigue in its rich Byzantine humus. Certainly, simplicity cannot survive long in it, or at least no longer than in any other great metropolis. Certainly, also, although the contrast between riches and poverty in Istanbul has been exaggerated, there is more attraction, temptation, envy and, therefore, intrigue in this city than in any other part of Turkey. To be deprived of a view or of access to the sea is all the more bitter for the magnificence of the land-scape; and while it is no hardship to be too poor to afford a meal in an Anatolian eating-house, the well-to-do who can afford to eat out in Istanbul restaurants are worthy objects of envy. However, when due allowance has been made for the uncharitableness of any metropolis, it is difficult to find particular fault with Istanbul – except in so far as it has fallen behind the times in the provision of public services, or in the appreciation of its own heritage. In a European sense, it became a provincial city after the proclamation of the Republic. With the departure of large numbers of non-Muslim middlemen (both in the commercial and the cultural sense) after the First World War, com-munication with Europe became for a time fitful, while there were shortages of technical and, above all, social skills. The Russian Revolu-tion, the inter-war economic crisis and the policy of nationalism and nationalization pursued by the republican government, had between them made of Istanbul a depressed city. However, since the last war many deficiencies have been made good and the city has grown not only in size but in vitality. But although richer than the rest of the country, it remains by European standards comparatively poor, and this is perhaps as it should be, for, in spite of its glittering past, Istanbul is part of the Turkish scene, for it shares most of the problems of the country, with which it is today in much closer communication than it has ever been before. However, while the range of Istanbul's influence is being extended, the old imbalance between the city and the country may be transformed into a regional imbalance. One can already see the beginnings of an Istanbul conurbation stretching from

148

Tekirdağ in the west to Izmit in the east, and economists have been predicting that the main economic and industrial activity of the country may revolve round the Ankara-Istanbul axis. Both cities already draw their power from a common electric grid, and with coal at Zongulduk, steel at Ereğli and Karabük, railway workshops at Eskişehir, textile factories at Bursa, all within easy reach of the Istanbul industrial complex, this prediction may well come true. However that may be, the development of Ankara as the official capital can now be seen to have introduced at least some regional diversification, and to have widened the central metropolitan area which otherwise would have been limited to Istanbul and its environs. So in spite of the heavy cost which it has imposed on the country, Atatürk's decision to move the seat of government to central Anatolia has improved the balance of the country and, therefore, brought stability to it. Moreover, with the development of communications – with a good road between Istanbul and Ankara, an improved railway service, several scheduled flights daily, telex and teleprinter lines – the disadvantages of having two centres are greatly mitigated.

Ankara is in central Anatolia, but not quite of it – the statement has to be qualified since the peasants who throng Ulus Square waiting for someone to hire them are clearly poor peasants from central Anatolia, which is itself one of the poorest parts of the country. Ankara, outside the small historic walled city in the shadow of the citadel, is modern. It is a planned city that bears witness to the limitations of planning. Originally meant for 100,000 people, it will soon reach the one million mark. Streets have had to be widened, trees planted at great cost have been uprooted, while small private houses are continually being pulled down to make room for large blocks. The architecture of official buildings has changed from the original colonial-oriental to severely functional. In a few cases this has achieved considerable dignity – such as the Atatürk mausoleum, built on a small hill that was a few years ago outside the city, but is now engulfed by it. Elsewhere there are obvious examples of official and private jerry-building. As usual, there are extensive shanty towns, in which more than half the population live. One unforeseen hazard has come from the widespread use of low-grade coal for central heating. In the winter, most of the city below the

Presidential Palace and the foreign embassies on Çankaya hill, is covered by a thick blanket of smog. However, life for the senior civil servant class and the foreign diplomats with whom they mix can be fairly agreeable. There are three universities, the headquarters of the Turkish Radio and Television Service, several minor local newspapers, a high-standard state theatre, opera, ballet and symphony orchestra, museums and galleries. But as befits a civil servant's city, the most absorbing pastime is politics and, of course, the struggle for promotion. On retirement, all those who can afford it move to more agreeable surroundings in Istanbul. As elsewhere in Turkey, there has been a great improvement in communications so that it is now easier to leave Ankara. This, in the hot Anatolian summer, is probably the prime need and, certainly, the hope of most of its inhabitants.

The Central Anatolian steppe country (the *bozkır*, or grey country as it is known in Turkish) stretches for miles to the east and south of Ankara, broken here and there by oases, usually at the foot of mountains from which they draw their water. It is in such oases and depressions that most of the cities are situated – the old Seljuk capital of Konya, Kayseri (Caesarea) at the foot of Mount Erciyeş (3,916 metres high) and the small market towns of Yozgat, Kırşehir, Nevşehir, Akşehir, Beyşehir, etc. This is the heart of historic Turkey, where Muslim Turks have formed the majority of the population for some eight centuries. For most of this time, it is true, they lived alongside smaller communities of Armenians and Greeks (thus in 1893 there were some 30,000 Armenians and 15,000 Greeks, alongside 85,000 Turks in Kayseri), but even these Christians spoke Turkish among themselves. Now they are all gone.

As in western Turkey, their departure created at first a shortage of skills which reduced economic activity. This has been remedied to some extent by the introduction of industries: there is a large textile factory at Kayseri, a big brewery at Yozgat, and large installations for extracting aluminium from local deposits of bauxite are being built with Soviet aid near Konya. Konya itself apart from being the centre of a fertile depression which, thanks to irrigation, has become one of the main granaries of Turkey, derives some profit from pilgrims and tourists who come to visit the tomb of Mevlânâ Jalaluddin Rumi, the poet and mystic who founded the order of whirling dervishes, known as Mevlevis. While this order remains officially banned together with the other dervish brotherhoods, secular displays of whirling are put on to attract tourists. Central and eastern Anatolia has much else to offer them: Seljuk architecture in great profusion everywhere, and above all in Konya, early Christian frescoes in the chapels carved out of limestone cones in the fantastic Göreme valley; mountaineering on Mount Erciyeş. The poverty of the countryside has in some cases engendered ingenuity. The merchants of Kayseri, in particular, are renowned for their cunning, apocryphally exemplified by their habit of introducing donkey-meat into sausages. For the peasants, who have fewer such opportunities of supplementing their incomes, emigration is often the only escape from poverty. A large proportion of the inhabitants of Ankara shanty towns, as well as of migrant Turkish workers in Western Europe, come from Central Anatolia which, in spite of economic development, remains the classic land of the peasant hardship described in the post-war protest literature. It is a land that exemplifies also the basic problems of Turkey: erosion, over-manning in agriculture, a shortage of capital and of skills in the villages, fragmentation of holdings, inadequate industrial development and, therefore, unemployment. These are problems that clamour for, but of their nature cannot be amenable to urgent solutions. Yet the fact that the problems persist and at time even seem to grow in size, should not blind us to the true nature of current development. This is that the country has been opened up, and while this opening up has exposed a great deal of poverty and misery, and by removing barriers round primitive villages, it has led to peasant migration and demographic imbalance, it has also allowed a gradual increase in technical and social skills. At the same time, hopes have been raised which neither current resources nor current skills can yet satisfy. Hope unfulfilled breeds discontent; it can also act as a spur to endeavour. In the last analysis, men, singly and collectively, are Turkey's greatest asset. The significance of the last few years' events is that all over Turkey the minds of men have been fired with a desire for betterment.

10   The economy

AT THE TIME of the last quinquennial census held in October 1965, the population of Turkey was approximately 31,400,000. It had increased over the preceding five years at the rate of 2·5 per cent per year. High as this rate was (for a comparison the population of the United Kingdom increased by 0·6 per cent per year between 1955 and 1965), it represented a decrease on the previous net rate of growth which, between 1955 and 1960 amounted to three per cent. While the size of families will decrease further as new city ideas spread throughout the country – and the government is lending a helping hand here by sponsoring campaigns for birth control – the absolute increase of population is bound to be large for many years to come.

Of the 25,664,000 Turks who were over six years old in 1965, forty-eight per cent were literate.

The working population in 1965 was 13,049,000. Of these 9,415,000 or seventy-two per cent were employed in agriculture. In 1955 this proportion was of the order of seventy-seven per cent, but in absolute terms there has been little change, for in 1955 (when the population of the country was, of course, smaller) employment in agriculture stood at 9,446,000. Employment is, incidentally, a very loose and sometimes misleading term, for a large number of these people often have very little work to do. However that may be, seventy-two per cent of the labour force produced in 1965 only thirty-seven per cent of the Gross National Product. But agricultural products accounted for some three-quarters of the country's exports: exports of cotton, tobacco and fruit and vegetables, each amounting to about one-fifth of the total. On the other hand, cereals and edible oils have had to be imported in consider-able although decreasing quantities in recent years. The worst year in this

152

respect was 1963 when thirteen per cent of the import bill went on foodstuffs, mainly cereals. Increasing the yield of cereals is one of the main problems facing Turkish agriculture.

About a third of the total area of Turkey is now cultivated. As we have seen, the cultivated area increased steadily in the 1950s largely at the expense of pastureland which between 1951 and 1964 decreased from thirty-seven to twenty-eight million hectares. However, yields per acre have been essentially stationary in the case of cereals, varying in other words only with weather conditions. If anything there has been a decrease since the peak of 1951–3 (when the Turkish yield of wheat stood at 1,200 kg. per hectare against an average of 1,730 kg. per hectare for all the countries in the Organization for European Economic Cooperation), a decrease due not only to adverse weather conditions but also to increasing erosion. On the other hand one can hope that with recent developments in irrigation, drainage, pest control, farming credits, mechanization and seed improvement, average yields will increase once again. Long-term trends in agriculture can often be masked by the short-term effect of weather. Yet improvements of agricultural services have been on such a large scale that they are bound to affect yields. In 1965 alone 15,000 new tractors came into service to join the 52,000 that were already in use so that the total number of tractors by now exceeds 70,000.

Until the 1960s almost no artificial fertilizer was used in Turkey (or to be exact less than 1 kg. per sown hectare, against 27 kg. in Greece and 467 kg. in Holland). In 1960, 176,000 tons of chemical fertilizer were used, in 1965, 766,000 tons (of which 400,000 tons were home-produced). A plan to spend $120 million on the production of artificial fertilizer was announced in 1966, when it was forecast that in 1967 consumption would reach 1,200,000 tons. A lot of work has also been done to improve land by irrigation and drainage. Thus the 1967 programme alone provided for the irrigation and drainage of over 140,000 hectares. If the 1963–7 Five-Year Plan target is achieved the proportion of irrigated land in the total cultivated area will have increased from four to over six per cent. These figures show both the extent of the progress achieved and the low level from which progress had to start. However, progress of this magnitude is bound to be reflected in production figures. While it is difficult to disentangle

153

short-term from long-term factors, the following figures suggest that considerable advances have already been made.

In 1962, 82,000 tons of tobacco were grown, 150,000 tons in 1966. The production of cotton increased from 245,000 tons in 1962 to 340,000 tons in 1966, that of tea from 37,000 tons in 1965 to 98,000 tons in 1966, that of oranges from 188,000 tons in 1962 to 300,000 tons in 1965. It is, of course, significant that all these figures refer to cash crops which are or can be exported. In the production of cereals it is still difficult to discern long-term trends. Depending on the weather the production of wheat has been fluctuating between 5 and 10 million tons, that of barley between 2 and 4 million, that of rice between 100,000 and 150,000 tons. In good years (1963, 1966) the total production of cereals approached 17 million tons; in average years it dropped to 14 million. However, to put it no higher, it would seem that the long-term effects of erosion, which were reflected in the drop in production after 1953, have now been counteracted.

In animal husbandry, increased marketing is the main long-term trend. As more animals and animal products are now being offered for sale (between 1964 and 1965 the increase amounted to over eight per cent) animal husbandry would seem to be moving out of a subsistence economy to a market economy. The number of goats of which Turkey had an estimated twenty-one million in 1963 has fortunately been decreasing; the horse and mule population has also been dropping, predictably because of the improvement in motor transport. As over-grazing is common, the decrease in the number of cattle and sheep should also be welcomed, but the general decrease in meat production suggests that decreased numbers have not been offset by increased weight and quality. In the meantime, exports of animals and animal products have been contributing $25 to 40 million a year to the country's earnings. Considering that pasturelands still cover some twenty-eight million hectares, two million more than tillage, production figures for home consumption and export remain very low.

The position is even worse in forestry, although here conservation measures are bound to have some effect. While animal husbandry accounted for one-third of the total value of agricultural production, forestry products amounted to only one per cent, although forests

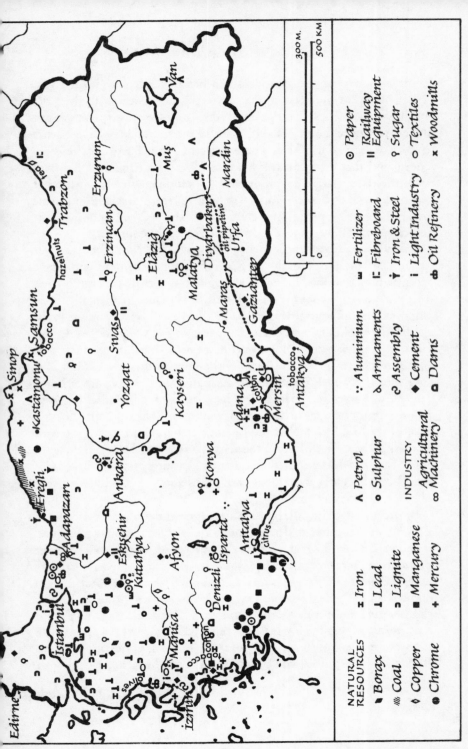

Economic map of Turkey

nominally cover an area of ten million hectares. But with fewer goats, less demand for firewood in the cities and, above all, with the strict application of forestry laws (under the constitution offences against these laws cannot be amnestied), Turkish forests probably have a better chance of survival than at any time in recent years. There are, however, complaints that derelict scrub-land has been designated as forest-land and, therefore, barred to productive agriculture, while contributing nothing useful to the economy. Attempts to return this land to private owners (all forests being publicly owned) have met with considerable resistance by self-appointed guardians of the public interest.

Manufactured and processed foods, which before the last war accounted for a negligible proportion of total consumption, have recently been gaining favour. We have seen earlier that margarine has become the staple cooking fat in towns. It is made, incidentally, from imported cheap vegetable oils, while Turkey exports its own high-quality olive oil. There are many more tinned foods offered for sale, but costs and prices are still high and traditional Turkish products and dishes reach the West not from Turkey but from Greece, Bulgaria, Rumania and Israel. Marketing of agricultural products both at home and abroad remains backward. The state often steps in to fix or to control retail prices, or to help in purchasing and distribution. There is a state Meat and Fish Marketing Board, a purchasing agency for cereals known as the Office of Soil Products; the state is the sole purchaser of sugar-beet and tea, and is the largest single purchaser of tobacco, for which (as for other traditional cash crops such as hazelnuts) it sets, in effect, a reserve price.

Before the 1950s the role of the state in agriculture was ambiguous. In Ottoman times the state derived much of its revenue from agriculture. The peasants paid tithes which often exceeded ten per cent of their production, a tax on domestic animals and other imposts. On the other hand state aid to agriculture was minimal. After the proclamation of the Republic, the state began to take less from agriculture, but at first did not give it appreciably more in return. Atatürk's most important relief measure was the abolition of tithes. The gap which they left in state revenue was, of course, a major factor limiting public investments. If Atatürk's Republic was a state too poor to undertake large-scale development projects, it was because it had decreased the exploitation of the peasants and not, like Communist Russia, increased it. Nevertheless, the taxes that remained – a tax on domestic animals, a road tax and a fisheries and game tax – bore down heavily on poor peasants. These taxes were often evaded, often collected forcibly by confiscation or the threat of imprisonment. They were much resented and most of them had to be repealed after the last war, when peasants' votes began to count and politicians tried to ingratiate themselves with the peasant electorate.

Just as agriculture was almost totally freed from taxation, price policy became a source of subsidies. During the Second World War, the government made use of the Office of Soil Products for the compulsory purchase of cereals needed to feed the cities and the army. It was at first, inevitably, an instrument of compulsion, if not of exploitation, for the prices paid to the peasants were kept low. Then, under the Menderes administration the role of the Office of Soil Products was transformed. Purchasing prices were repeatedly increased, partly, it was alleged, in order to buy the peasants' support for the Menderes Democratic Party. The state began to subsidize agriculture by purchasing agricultural products at inflated prices, as well as by giving the peasants more credits, while at the same time undertaking large-scale land improvement and support services. But just as Atatürk's refusal to squeeze the peasants had limited the ability to industrialize the country, so Menderes' policy of subsidizing the peasants meant that there were inadequate domestic savings to pay for development. As large-scale development nevertheless occurred, it predictably led to inflation. In the end, inflation overtook price increases paid to the peasants. Although Menderes' successors have promised to avoid these mistakes, further price increases have had to be paid in recent years. More and more, the state has had to step in with reserve prices and support purchasing to protect the peasants from the full effects of over-production (as in the case of tobacco, tea and hazelnuts) or falling demand. At the same time more money has been spent on agricultural services. Today the state contributes more to agriculture than it has ever done before. To offset this expenditure, agricultural incomes have been made subject to income tax, but the exemption level has been set so high by Turkish standards that the tax yields very little revenue. It is true, of course, that direct taxation is a minor source of revenue in Turkey (in the 1967 budget, for example, direct taxes amounted only to TL 4,430 million out of a total revenue of TL 18,313 million), but even indirect taxation does not hit the peasants too hard, since they are not major consumers of manufactured goods, with the exception of tobacco, sugar, cotton goods and now petrol for tractors. It is impossible to estimate to what extent indirect taxes are borne by the peasants, but in 1967 the profits earned and taxes paid by the state monopolies accounted for twelve per cent of revenue, and even if one adds the tax paid on petrol used in tractors, and production taxes on the manufac- tured goods consumed in the countryside, the total in unlikely to exceed a third of total state revenue.

Since, as we have seen, seventy-two per cent of the working popula- tion are engaged in agriculture, it follows that the state has become an instrument of redistribution on behalf of the countryside – which is perhaps as it should be since city businessmen usually owe their living to the efforts of the peasants. In spite, however, of state aid which, coming as it does in the shape of support purchasing and small credits, is spread out thinly, agriculture remains very short of capital. And capital, as well as technical skills, is what it needs if it is to realize its immense potential. The example of post-war Greece which has much more limited land resources, although of course, it supports a much smaller population, and where an admittedly mistaken policy of subsidies has led to an over-production of cereals, suggests that Turkey too could easily produce more than enough cereals, as well as adding fresh and tinned fruit and vegetables and wine to its traditional exports of dry fruit, cotton and tobacco. If present trends continue this develop- ment should be taking place in the next few years. But although at the present time state support of Turkish agriculture is inadequate, this fact should not obscure the major change that has occurred in Turkey. The state, which as in most backward agricultural countries, has always exploited the peasants, has become, through the workings of democracy, a redistributive state.

Asia Minor has always been known as a land rich in minerals. Iron, copper, lead, gold, silver, mercury and sulphur have been mined there throughout recorded history. A few of the mines which are still

158

worked today – like the copper mines at Ergani Maden in southeastern Anatolia – have been in existence for centuries. Others – like the famous silver mines at Gümüşane in northern Turkey – are now exhausted. When the Republic was proclaimed, the production of minerals was small and much of it was in foreign hands. Although many mines were nationalized, private mining including a few foreign concessions continues. Between the wars the production of coal (at the Zonguldak coalfield on the Black Sea coast) and of copper was increased, and the state did a great deal of prospecting. Rapid development in mining came only after the last war. The production of coal went up from less than 4 million tons at the end of the war to over 7 million tons in 1966, of lignite (low-grade brown coal) from some half a million to over 6 million tons, of copper from 20,000 to 26,000 tons, of boracite from 3,000 to some 170,000 tons, of chrome ore from under 100,000 to nearly 700,000 tons. (All these figures refer to ungraded pithead production.) In addition, approximately 1,600,000 tons of iron ore were produced in 1966. New minerals were added to the list. Production of bauxite started in the 1960s and in 1967 an agreement was signed with the Soviet Union for the construction of a factory near Konya, in central Turkey, capable of producing 200,000 tons of alumina or 60,000 tons of pure aluminium a year. Under another agreement, the Russians were to build a plant to process 40,000 tons of copper from mines in the Black Sea region. In 1966 very rich deposits of iron ore were discovered near Anamur, roughly opposite the Cyprus coast.

Oil prospecting began in Turkey in 1932, with the first significant discovery at Ramandağ (near Batman) made in 1946. However, in 1954 oil production was only 60,000 tons a year. Later, foreign companies were given prospecting titles and in 1966 some two million tons of crude oil were produced (and a further three million tons imported). All the petroleum products used in Turkey are at present refined in the country, the three refineries (at Batman, Mersin and Izmit) having an annual capacity of about five million tons. A fourth refinery at Izmir and extensions to existing refineries are planned to increase capacity to ten million tons a year by 1970.

The consumption of electric energy which, at the end of the last war, stood at some 5 million kW/hr. increased more than tenfold in twenty years, exceeding 5 billion kW/hr. in 1966. But even when the current programme of building is completed and the dams at Keban on the Euphrates, Gökçekaya on the Sakarya and Kadıncık in the Taurus mountains, start generating electricity, Turkey will have the lowest consumption of electricity per head of population in Europe. In 1966 consumption per head in Turkey was only 164 kW/hr. (U.K. over 3,000 kW/hr.). This means in effect that the vast majority of Turkish villages still have no electricity.

Production of iron and steel started in Turkey just before the war when a first mill was built at Karabük in western Turkey. In 1964 a second complex was added at Ereğli on the Black Sea coast, while iron and steel were also produced at the arms factory at Kırıkkale near Ankara and on a small scale in Istanbul and Izmir. In 1966, 736,000 tons of pig iron, 842,000 tons of steel ingots and 216,000 tons of sheets and pipes were produced. In view of increasing consumption, plans were made to build a third iron and steel complex, this time in southern Turkey.

Turkey is more or less self-sufficient in a number of other 'intermediate' goods, such as cement, paper and glass. Cement production which stood at some 300,000 tons a year at the end of the war, increased to over two million tons in 1960 and then approached four million tons in 1966. By the end of the second Five-Year Plan in 1972 it should reach 10 million tons. Production of glass stood at 35,000 tons in 1966, having risen from 14,000 tons in 1960. The production of paper has also more than doubled in the 'sixties reaching 106,000 tons in 1966, when work began on two more paper factories in addition to the one at present operating at Izmit near Istanbul.

As far as consumer goods are concerned, Turkey's industrialization started with textiles and sugar in the 1930s. However, production and consumption of both commodities were low until after the last war. In the 1950s production capacity for sugar was increased to the point where it was in excess of demand and attempts were made to export Turkish sugar. This proved possible, but the sugar was sold at a loss. In 1966 approximately 600,000 tons of sugar were produced. Textile capacity is also adequate, production being governed by demand. In 1965 Turkey produced some 600 million metres of cotton fabrics and

24 million metres of woollen fabrics. In 1966 work also began on installations to make man-made fibres. At the same time first steps were taken to produce plastics for industrial use.

One recent development has been the rapid increase in the assembly of manufactured goods. Cars, lorries, tractors, diesel locomotives, buses, refrigerators, typewriters, record players, radios, tape-recorders and many other consumer durables are now assembled in Turkey. All these products have to have a specified content of local components. In the case of vehicles the proportion works out at forty to fifty per cent including steel chassis, tyres, batteries, etc. Almost all the medicines and drugs that are needed are produced locally under licence by Turkish firms or by foreign firms with manufacturing facilities in Turkey.

The growth of Turkish industry has been favoured by a policy of tax concessions, as well as by protective custom tariffs and import quotas, a policy which started before the last war with the passing of the Law for the Encouragement of Industry. On the other hand industrial growth has been held back by shortages of capital, which were only partly made good when a Law for the Encouragement of Foreign Capital was passed after the war. Protection is not, of course, the best way of promoting efficiency, particularly when technical, administrative and, generally, social skills are short, as they inevitably are in a developing country. The initial advantage of low labour costs was not usually reflected in production costs which tended to be high by Western standards. However, in recent years efficiency has been improved by a growing technical and administrative knowledge, as well as by efforts to make state enterprises meet their own costs without relying on Treasury subsidies. This policy has been conspicuously unsuccessful in railway finance, but then Turkey is not the only country which has to subsidize its railways. However, in Turkey the decline of the railways started only after the last war. In 1946 the railways were still making a profit of TL fifteen million a year (then roughly worth £2 million).

At that time, there were less than 10,000 motor vehicles of all types on Turkish roads. And although Turkish records for 1946 showed some 13,000 kms of 'macadam roads in good condition' and 12,813 kms of 'graded earth roads', only a small proportion of the network was suitable for motor transport. On the other hand, in July 1966 there were 275,000 motor vehicles, and according to a more realistic assessment, the total length of roads amount to 60,000 kms of which 35,000 kms were usable in all weathers, but only 13,000 kms had a proper tarmac surface. The sudden influx of motor vehicles in a society that had no experience of modern machines led, of course, to an alarming accident rate, Turkey having one of the worst records in the world in road safety, calculated on a vehicle-km basis. In the meantime, the railway network, whose extension had been the major economic achievement of the Republic between the two world wars, and which was 7,585 kms long in 1946, was further lengthened to over 8,000 kms by 1967. The new lines were mainly in eastern Anatolia. There were also many technical improvements: passenger and freight cars and diesel locomotives are now manufactured in Turkey, the introduction of diesel services has cut down travelling times (at the end of the war the Istanbul–Ankara 'express' still took some 16 hours to cover the 400-odd kilometres between the two cities), one Istanbul suburban line was electrified, and plans were drawn up for the first major electrification project between Ankara and the coal port of Zonguldak.

The gross tonnage of the Turkish merchant fleet increased from approximately 200,000 tons at the end of the war to over 670,000 tons in 1966, a little more than half of the total being owned by private firms and the rest by the state shipping lines. Shipping has been favoured by post-war work on the harbours of Istanbul, Zonguldak, Trabzon, Izmir, Mersin and Iskenderun.

The state airlines (THY) operate an extensive and reasonably efficient internal network, on which they managed to make a profit in 1966, although fares remained cheap. So far, however, Turkish airlines have been too short of modern aircraft to claim a significant share of international air traffic. Turkey has two international airports, at Istanbul and Ankara. A third one will be added to the list when the American air base near Izmir is turned over to civilian use.

How to ensure good management of the state economic enterprises remains the basic problem of the Turkish economy. They provide about half the country's industrial and mining production. They produce almost all the energy. They operate the railways, airlines and half the shipping fleet. They have a large share in banking. With the exception of the railways and shipping, most of them had succeeded by 1966 in earning a small profit in their operations, but they remained unable either to service their capital debts or to find investment capital otherwise than by recourse to Treasury loans. This has inevitably led to mistakes in capital outlay. The economic weakness of the state economic enterprises is reflected in their relatively small share of the country's foreign trade. In 1965, seventy per cent of the imports and eighty-seven per cent of the exports were handled by private firms.

Like most developing countries, Turkey has had since the last war a persistent deficit in its foreign trade. The size of this deficit is governed by the availability of foreign credits and grants. Between 1947 and 1950 the deficit was $45 million a year; in the ten years of Mr Menderes' administration, between 1950 and 1960, it rose to approximately $100 million a year; and between 1960 and 1966 it averaged almost $200 million a year. In 1966, when economic activity was particularly lively, imports amounted to $725 million and exports to $490 million, the deficit, incidentally, being smaller than had been planned. The orientation of Turkish trade remains solidly Western, although the share of Communist countries and particularly of the Soviet Union has been rising. Nevertheless, in 1966 the Soviet Union still took less than four per cent of Turkish exports, and provided only some 3·5 per cent of the country's imports.

Foreign trade deficits were of course a reflection of investments and industrialization, and they grew as Turkey's economic growth rate increased. The two post-war development plans, covering the years 1963–72, provided for seven per cent growth. Achievement so far has been below this level, largely because progress in agriculture has been slower than expected. On the other hand, the growth of industry in the three years 1964–6 has been above eight per cent per year. When, therefore, the present investments in agriculture begin to bear fruit, as they inevitably will, Turkey's economic progress, which is already considerable, may well reach the level of what has been loosely termed an economic miracle.

The long-term prospects of the Turkish economy are excellent. The country has a large and increasingly healthy labour force; technical knowledge and adaptability are improving; social habits which must be acquired before a technological society can begin to function are spreading. Natural resources are adequate, where they are not ample. The country does or can produce almost all the raw materials and energy which it needs. However, economic development often seems to depend on imponderables, more precisely on social and human qualities which are difficult to calculate and more difficult to change. It has been argued that what has held back Turkey was oriental or Islamic 'lethargy', contentment with things as they are, even fatalism. It has also been argued that the Turks, as a nation of soldiers and peasants, are unsuited to trade and industry. Habits and traditions should not, of course, be underestimated, but the experience of recent years has shown that the Turks desire to better their lot, and also that they can acquit themselves perfectly well in modern industry, although less so in trade. What is more, while presumed disabilities have been usually shown to be non-existent, some traditional qualities have in fact stood the Turks in good stead.

The tradition of discipline, for example, has made Turkey a more stable country than most of its neighbours. The experience of government, acquired over centuries in an extensive empire, has engendered a seriousness and a knowledge of the practical difficulties of administration, which have so far kept Turkish governments away from ideological extremes or which have at least moderated the flights of fancy of armchair rulers and advisers. It has been encouraging to see the Turkish government rejecting the advice of progressive Western economists and thus sparing themselves the troubles of certain under-developed and occasionally even developed countries, which have been less cautious in their experiments. But one should not claim too much. Turkey could well do with more administrative continuity, with less legislation and better implementation of existing laws, with fewer regulations and more common sense. Above all, the growth of the Turkish economy depends on such non-economic factors as continued political stability and increased individual freedom.

Conclusion

IT IS APPARENTLY THE CASE that where families are poorly fed, the strongest children – the children, that is, with the greatest growth potential – are the first to fall sick. When taken care of and properly nourished, they usually outstrip their brothers or sisters in height, weight and other physical qualities. It is not perhaps too fanciful to see in these findings of medical research a parallel with the recent history of Turkey. Turkey's remarkable vitality today – the growth of its population, their enthusiasm for betterment, their appetite for freedom – suggests that the sick man's sickness had been largely due to deprivation. He had been bled white by wars, starved of practical knowledge, maltreated by doctors who, while themselves impoverishing his environment, attempted to change his constitution, instead of providing him with the means to heal him.

The recovery of the Turkish nation was accomplished in two stages. In the first, it won for itself an adequate territory in which it could live and multiply. The victory won under Atatürk's leadership in the War of Independence between 1918 and 1922 gave the Turks the possibility of growth. But growth itself did not gather speed until after the Second World War, when the restraints on the Turks' energies were gradually removed, while the isolation in which the defence of their territory had placed them was ended, intercourse with wealthier nations was resumed and the lessons and fruits of progress in Western lands were to some extent applied for the improvement of Turkey.

Turkey is today undergoing the most rapid and the most extensive changes in its history. Change is everywhere – in the growth of the population, of literacy, of industry, of communications, in the diversification of employment for women, in internal and external migrations, in the break-up of the old patriarchial, extended family. The strain of these changes is also everywhere evident. A society breaks its ranks when it marches forward: some people, some classes, some regions are luckier, or more industrious, or better endowed than others. And although it can be argued that in the present phase of Turkey's growth, the rich are getting richer, while the poor are at worst not getting any poorer and at best getting richer themselves, the inevitable disparity in rewards breeds jealousy and even hatred. The brotherhood of Muslims was, for a long time, based on shared misery. Today, when a growing stream of people escape from this common misery, they often lack any sense of concern for those who are less fortunate. In Turkey today a political conscience is more apparent than a social or a moral conscience. Traditions, which governments were once often powerless to change, are today dying naturally in the changed environment of a new technological society. Given the impersonal machinery of a modern society, the achievement of personal and social balance requires more than nationalism, which Atatürk sought to substitute for Islam as a source of cohesive inspiration. When a move to town, or even success in town – a proper house, modern amenities, even a car – fail to bring contentment, nationalism is powerless to help.

To ease the discomfort of change, radical remedies have been suggested: socialism seen as complete planning, nationalism seen as an answer to a presumed conspiracy of foreigners, a revival of religious discipline, if not of the spirit of Islam. There is personal maladjustment and also group maladjustment. The old educated élite looks askance at the rising lower middle class. Civil servants expect more respect than they get or perhaps than they deserve. The officer corps, educated apart from the rest of the people, set apart in their way of life, are searching for a role commensurate with their numbers and self-importance. They were, they believe, not only the defenders of the Fatherland, but also the promoters of social progress. Progress has now led to unfamiliar territory, where enterprise is at least as valuable as discipline, and where consent must replace constraint. Moreover one can no longer assume that all officers think alike – that divisions in society have not affected the armed forces. The problem of the armed forces – of their uncertain role in society, of their burden on the economy – is not the problem of NATO membership. NATO has saved Turkey large sums in foreign exchange, which would otherwise have had to be paid for modern arms. Closer familiarity with the British and American tradition of assigning to the armed forces a subordinate function in an essentially civilian society may also have done some good.

In most countries bordering on Turkey, technological change had led to civil strife and was consummated only after the upheaval of war. In Russia, the Balkans, Italy and Spain the kind of change which Turkey is undergoing today, could not be accomplished peacefully. But then in these countries local strife was exacerbated by foreign wars and foreign antagonisms. Turkey is luckier. On the whole the outside world has been helping Turkish development instead of aggravating the country's problems. True, East–West rivalry is reflected in Turkey, but since Stalin's death, the Soviet Union and other Communist countries have thought more in terms of winning over Turkish governments than of undermining them. With Turkish stability being helped by the West, while not being seriously threatened by the East, the country's cohesive forces have a better chance of coping with the effects of social and economic change. Consolation can also be drawn from the fact that the coup of 1960 has been, in terms of social upheaval, a mild one, and that by demonstrating both the limitations of revolutionary zeal and the importance of stability, it may have served as a vaccination against a more serious attack.

Dangers remain in plenty – the strains and tensions that have been outlined earlier, adventitious issues such as that of Cyprus, whose destructive potential is wholly out of proportion to its intrinsic merit, faults of statesmanship, when basically moderate politicians seek tactical advantage from appeals to social jealousy, or xenophobia, forces that, if roused sufficiently, could easily overwhelm them and the whole country. In the economy too, faults of management that in the West would cost a government the loss of a by-election or, at most, of the general elections, could in Turkey provide an opportunity for all those who despair of democracy, more in hope than in sorrow. But just as NATO may perhaps exert a steadying influence on the armed forces, so here too organizations such as the Aid to Turkey Consortium of the Organization of Economic Cooperation and Development, not only provide aid but can also serve as a brake on mistaken policies. Finally, whatever the tensions and provocations, there is before the mass of literate Turks the example of the industrial West on whose doorstep they live and which they find wholly admirable. And the West today is, as we all know, pragmatic in its attitude, believing above all that it is unwise to upset the apple-cart, even if one favours the equal distribution of apples.

In Turkey the planners have defined their objective as 'development in stability and social justice'. It is a worthy but a difficult task, particularly as development can in the short run endanger stability, while, in an imperfect world, the provision of social justice by too zealous a government can put an end to development. However, there is no insuperable reason why the highest common factor of development, stability and social justice should not be achieved in Turkey. Certainly nothing that has happened in the last few years makes one despair of the future, while there is much to give one hope. And for those who may have reservations about the value of develop-ment, there is consolation in the fact that however rapidly Turkey is changing today, there is much that is unchanged and perhaps some aspects that are unchangeable. That rapid change is the dominant trend in Turkey cannot be denied. But to define a trend is not to describe the average. If, for example, school enrolment has been increasing at a vertiginous rate, it remains nonetheless true that education in Turkey is less like a pyramid and more like a minaret rising from a long low building, since the vast majority of the population never get beyond the primary school. One can, similarly, stress at will either the growth of industry or its comparatively small size, recent progress in road-building or the fact that there are still large tracts of the country that are inaccessible, advances in scientific husbandry or the undeniable fact that most of agriculture is still primitive, the growth of initiative or the persistence of paternalism, the growth of tourism or the fact that most of the country, including some of its most beautiful spots, remains innocent of tourists. Most significantly, one can stress either the progress towards a technological society, or the obvious fact that by-and-large, in their outlook, their philosophy, their personal and social relations, their virtues and their vices, the mass of Turks lead lives and are governed by habits that are out of tune with the demands of technology and that are sometimes all the better for being so. So too, while most Turks desire the prosperity that has been achieved in Europe, they would not go so far as to say that their country is already part of Europe or even feel comfortable if it were. American sociologists who have recently been applying their slide-rules to Turkish education came to the conclusion that, as a partially developed country, Turkey stood on 'Level II of a four-level classification of development'.[30] This is one way of looking at Turkey. In 1967 the Chief of the Turkish General Staff, Cemal Tural took another view. 'We are not a nation that can be expressed in calculations and statistics,' he said, adding, 'If we can bring up the coming generation in peace, we shall become a nation that will count in the world.' And in fact peace remains today the key to progress, as it was when Atatürk first defined his policy as 'peace at home and peace abroad.'

Note on spelling and pronunciation

Modern Turkish spelling has been used, except where an accepted English spelling exists. However the dot on the capital I has been omitted. It is difficult to be consistent and easy to be pedantic in the matter. As modern Turkish spelling is phonetic, words should be pronounced as written. The following points should be kept in mind. Vowels have 'continental' (i.e. non-diphthongized) open values. Ö and ü are pronounced as in German. The undotted 'i' (like the Polish 'y' and Russian ы) represents an intermediate sound, which bears a distant affinity to the short vowel which can sometimes be discerned between the 'b' and 'l' of 'table'. Consonants are pronounced as in English, except that:

c   stands for j in jam.
ç   stands for ch in church.
g   is always hard as in gas.
ğ   is not pronounced but lengthens the preceding vowel.
j   as in French, or s in measure.
ş   stands for sh in ship.
y   is always a consonant as in yellow.

The circumflex (ˆ) lengthens a vowel and palatalizes (softens) the consonants g, k and l which precede it.

Notes on the text

INTRODUCTION

1 M. A. L. F. Alix, *Précis de l'histoire de l'Empire Ottoman* (Paris, 1822) I, i.

I HISTORICAL TURKEY

2 Vicomte de la Jonquière, *Histoire de l'Empire Ottoman* (Paris, 1881) 30, 51.
3 John Schiltberger, a contemporary eye-witness, quoted in *Encyclopaedia of Islam* (second edition), article on Bursa.

2 THE OTTOMAN BACKGROUND

4 In a proclamation to the Greeks, issued on 22 March 1711, Peter the Great of Russia said, '. . . and I shall show to you the same respect that the great *efendis* (Ottoman civil servants) and the great *aghas* (Ottoman commanders and landlords) have shown to you'. Quoted in Paulos Carolides, *Historia tes Hellados* (Athens, 1925) 596.
5 de la Jonquière, 34.
6 Population statistics are analysed in Altan Deliorman, 'Birinci Cihan Savaşının sonuna kadar Makedonya'da Türk Nüfusu Meselesi' in *Türk Kültürü* (Ankara, 1965–6) No. 33, 589–93; No. 39, 246–53.
7 Quoted by Colin L. Smith, *The Embassy of Sir William White at Constantinople* (O.U.P. 1957) 106.
8 Alix, I, lvi–lvii.
9 de la Jonquière, 628.

3 DEFEAT AND VICTORY

10 These figures which are taken from the Ottoman census of 14 March 1914, are quoted by Sabahattin Selek, *Anadolu Ihtilâlic* (Istanbul, 1963) I, 50–1.
11 Ibid. I, 84, 92.
12 Ibid. I, 92–3.

13 Ibid. I, 13.
14 Ibid. I, 288.
15 Ibid. I, 92.
16 Turkish National Commission for UNESCO, *Atatürk* (Ankara, 1963) 118.
17 Niyazi Berkes, *The Development of Secularism in Turkey* (McGill, 1964) 189–90.
18 Bernard Lewis, *The Emergence of Modern Turkey* (O.U.P., 1961) 128.

4 THE REPUBLIC OF ATATÜRK
19 UNESCO, *Atatürk,* 171.
20 General Directorate of Statistics, *Small Statistical Abstract of Turkey,* No. 291 (Ankara, 1948) 335.
21 Orhan Kemal, *Baba Evi* (Istanbul, 1949) 79–80.
22 Lord Kinross, *Atatürk* (London, 1964) 482, 486.

7 THE PEOPLE: UNITY AND DIVERSITY
23 Dr Mübeccel Kiray, *Ereğli Ağır Sanayiden Önce Bir Sahil Kasabası* (Ankara, 1964) 184.
24 Ibid. 186–7.
25 CHP Araştırma ve Yayin Bürosu, *Ziraatimizin Bugünkü Meseleleri* (Ankara, 1961) 6.

9 THE COUNTRY
26 S. N. Matveyev, *Turtsiya, Fiziko-Geograficheskoye Opisaniye* (Moscow, 1946) 140.
27 G. E. Bean, *Aegean Turkey* (London, 1966) 219.
28 Christiansen-Weniger quoted by S. N. Matveyev, op. cit., 63.

CONCLUSION
29 Andreas M. Kazamias, *Education and the Quest for Modernity in Turkey* (London, 1966) 181.

Select Bibliography

There has always been a vast literature on Turkey in English, but until recently the number of scholarly and reliable studies has been very small. However, since the last war the situation has improved, so that the reader who wishes to find out more about Turkey can be directed to a number of first-class studies based on a mass of new material.

A complete bibliography of books on Turkey published to date will be found in J. K. Birge, *A Guide to Turkish Area Study*, Washington 1949. Since then there have been two one-volume general introductions to Turkey: Nuri Eren, *Turkey Today – and Tomorrow. An Experiment in Westernization*, London 1963, and Geoffrey Lewis, *Turkey*, 3rd Ed., London 1965.

There is still no satisfactory one-volume history of Turkey. However, the organization of the Ottoman Empire and its decadence, and the process which culminated in the emergence of modern Turkey are well documented. The reader interested in Turkish history should start with P. Wittek's epoch-making short study *The Rise of the Ottoman Empire*, Royal Asiatic Society Monograph no. 23, London 1936; go on with Dorothy M. Vaughan's *Europe and the Turk. A Pattern of Alliances 1350–1700*, Liverpool U.P. 1954, for diplomatic history; and for the internal organization of the classical Ottoman State refer to H. A. R. Gibb and Harold Bowen, *Islamic Society and the West*, i: *Islamic Society in the Eighteenth Century*, pt 1, London 1950. Pt 2, London 1957.

The standard work on the modernization process is Bernard Lewis' *The Emergence of Modern Turkey*, O.U.P. 1961. Readers interested in Turkish political thought during that process can also refer to Niyazi Berkes, *The Development of Secularism in Turkey*, McGill 1964, and E. J. Rosenthal, *Islam in the Modern National State*, C.U.P. 1965. There are several excellent monographs on pre-Republican modern Turkish history: Şerif Mardin, *The*

173

Genesis of Young Turkish Thought, Princeton 1962; Robert Devereux, *The First Ottoman Constitutional Period,* Baltimore 1963; and E. E. Ramsaur, *The Young Turks. Prelude to the Revolution of 1908,* Princeton 1957.

When we come to the Republican period, the best biography of Atatürk is undoubtedly Lord Kinross', *Atatürk: The Rebirth of a Nation,* London 1964. For contemporary political history, refer to Richard Robinson, *The First Turkish Republic: A Case Study in National Development,* Cambridge, Mass. 1963 and Kemal Karpat, *Turkey's Politics: The Transition to a Multi-Party System,* Princeton 1959. A convenient summary of modern diplomatic history will be found in Altemur Kiliç, *Turkey and the World,* Washington 1959.

Documentation on various aspects of modern Turkey is also increasing. For the economy, the standard works are: M. W. Thornburg *et al., Turkey, An Economic Appraisal,* New York 1949, and Z. Y. Herschlag, *Turkey: An Economy in Transition,* The Hague n.d. (preface dated 1958). For education, a recent study is Andreas Kazamias, *Education and the Quest for Modernity in Turkey,* London 1966. Finally, readers interested in sociology should refer to Paul Stirling, *Turkish Village,* London 1965.

Books on language and literature are also available. If the reader wishes to learn some Turkish, he can begin with Geoffrey Lewis' *Teach Yourself Turkish,* London 1959, and acquire at the same time the one-volume concise Oxford Turkish Dictionary, ed. A. D. Alderson and Fahir Iz, O.U.P. 1959. Some translations of Turkish literature are available: Ottoman poetry is well served in E. J. W. Gibb's monumental six-volume *History of Ottoman Poetry,* London 1900-9, while for modern poets there is only Derek Patmore's slim volume *The Star and the Crescent,* London 1946. There are at least three modern Turkish novels in translation: Yaşar Kemal's *Mehmed, My Hawk* (tr. Edouard Roditi, London 1961) and *The Wind From the Plain* (tr. Thilda Kemal, London 1963); and Reşat Nuri Güntekin's *The Autobiography of a Turkish Girl* (tr. Sir Wyndham Deedes, London 1949). The late Sir Wyndham Deedes has also translated Mahmut Makal's plea for reforms in the villages, under the title *A Village in Anatolia* (ed. Paul Stirling, London 1954). However, the short stories of Sait Faik and of Orhan Kemal – which are among the best products of contemporary Turkish literature – still await a translator.

Who's Who

ABDUL AZIZ (Abdülaziz) (1830–76) Ottoman Sultan, acceded to the throne in 1861. His reign witnessed a number of reforms (new provisions for provincial administration, new judicial organs, educational reforms including founding of first university in Istanbul) but also a large number of nationalist revolts in the Balkans and in Greece, and, finally the bankruptcy of Ottoman finances, which was probably the proximate cause of the Sultan's deposition and suicide. In 1867 Abdul Aziz was the first Ottoman Sultan to visit Christian Europe as a friendly head of state.

ABDÜLHAK HAMID (1852–1937) Turkish poet and dramatist. He has been described variously as a follower of Shakespeare, Corneille, Racine and Victor Hugo. He was in fact a cultured Ottoman diplomat who liked the classics which he saw in Western theatre and tried to give Turkish literature a similar repertoire. In his time he was considered a daring innovator; today most Turks would rather read about him than read him.

ABDUL HAMID II (Abdülhamid) (1842–1918) Antepenultimate Ottoman Sultan, he succeeded to the throne in 1876, under the wing of the reformist grand vizier Midhat Pasha, who had played an important part in the deposition, on the grounds of madness, of Abdul Hamid's elder brother the Sultan Murad V. The first two years of his reign witnessed the victorious conclusion of the war against Serbia and Montenegro; a Great Powers' conference in Istanbul at which Russia demanded that the Ottomans should abandon the fruits of victory and, generally, submit to their dictation; the proclamation of the first Ottoman Constitution; the meeting and the prorogation for thirty years of the first Ottoman Parliament and, worst of all, the disastrous war with Russia in 1877–8 which lost the Ottoman Empire, Bulgaria, Bosnia, Thessaly and Cyprus as well as provinces in eastern Turkey which were to revert to the Turkish State in 1921. However, after this defeat, for which he was not

responsible, Abdul Hamid succeeded by skilful diplomacy, careful management of resources and some improvement in administration and education, in
postponing by thirty-two years the loss of the Ottoman possessions in Europe,
and in 1897 he was even allowed by the Great Powers to beat the Greeks
(although not to derive any benefit from his victory). In 1908 young officers
who thought that they could manage the Empire better, forced him to reconvene
Parliament and in April 1909, when privates and NCO's in the Istanbul
garrison mutinied against the Young Turkish officers, Abdul Hamid was
deposed for having allegedly encouraged the mutiny, and was exiled to
Salonica. Three years later that city was lost by the Young Turks to the Greeks
and Abdul Hamid was hurriedly transferred back to Istanbul, to die in a
palace on the Bosporus. In spite of constant nationalist agitation and consequent
troubles, his reign was both more prosperous and less sanguinary than those of
his immediate successors.

ABDUL MEJID I (Abdülmecid) (1823–61) Ottoman Sultan. He succeeded
his father Mahmud II in 1839. His accession was followed by the Reform
Edict of 1839 (known also as the Tanzimat Charter) which proclaimed the
inviolability of the life and property of all Ottoman subjects, and by practical
reforms in the administration, the army, education etc. Although there were
also the usual revolts and financial troubles, Abdul Mejid's reign briefly held
out the promise that the Ottoman Empire, particularly after its alliance with
Britain and France and subsequent victory over the Russians in the Crimean
War of 1853–6, might be stabilized and accepted as a European multi-national
power.

ABDUL MEJID II (Abdülmecid) (1868–1944) First and last Ottoman
Caliph without temporal powers. He was elected to this curious office by the
Turkish Grand National Assembly in November 1922 and dismissed and
exiled in March 1924. His brief pseudo-spiritual reign did not (and was not
meant by Atatürk to) delay the secularization of the new republican Turkish
state.

ALPARSLAN (c. 1030–73) Seljuk Sultan. In 1063 he succeeded his uncle
Tughril Beg, the first of the Great Seljuks. The following year he captured the
old Armenian capital of Ani and the city of Kars – both today in eastern
Turkey – and ensured the submission of the kingdom of Georgia. He returned
to the same region in 1071 to defeat the Byzantine army under Emperor
Romanos Diogenes at the battle of Malazgirt. After Malazgirt the whole of

Asia Minor lay open to conquest and, more important, settlement by the Sultan's Turkomans and other Muslims who came in their wake.

ATATÜRK MUSTAFA KEMAL (1881–1936) Founder and first President of Turkish Republic. Born in Salonica, he entered the local military preparatory school at the age of twelve and spent the subsequent thirty years in, and finally at the head of, the Turkish army. Commissioned 1902, promoted Staff Captain 1905, involved in young officers' plots against Sultan Abdul Hamid (q.v.), posted to Damascus 1906, promoted A/Major 1907, transferred to Salonica in the same year, took some part in preparation of Young Turkish military coup of July 1908; appointed Chief of Staff of Strike Army sent from Macedonia to suppress military mutiny in Istanbul in April 1909, Chief of Staff of Ottoman forces operating against Albanian rebels in 1910, promoted Major 1911, active service against Italians in Libya 1912, appointed Military Attaché in Sofia 1913, promoted Lt. Col. 1914, posted to Dardanelles 1915 where he held British advance, was promoted Colonel and given command of a vital sector where he organized a successful counter-attack, largely instru-mental in determining the failure of the whole Allied operation; promoted Brigadier General 1916 and posted to Eastern front where he won back two towns from the Russians; posted to Palestine front in 1917 as Commander of 7th Army; accompanied Crown Prince Mehmed Vahdettin to Germany in December 1917, returning to the Palestine front in January 1918; effected withdrawal of his units to a line north of Aleppo where he organized resistance until the armistice in October 1918; briefly Commander of Ottoman forces on Syrian front, before returning to Istanbul where he attempted to organize Turkish national resistance against the country's planned partition; appointed Inspector of Ottoman 9th Army in Eastern Turkey in 1919, organized nationalist congress in Erzurum, resigned commission, organized congress in Sivas, was elected Chairman of Permanent Executive Committee, elected Deputy for Erzurum, moved to Ankara, organized the meeting in Ankara in April 1920 of the new Legislature, the Turkish Grand National Assembly which elected him President. Appointed C-in-C of Turkish national forces by the Assembly in 1921, held the Greeks in vital battle of Sakarya, and was given rank of Marshal and title of *Ghazi*; inflicted final defeat on the Greeks in August 1922. Formed People's Party in 1923, was elected Deputy in Second Assembly, and President of the Assembly. Obtained the proclamation of the Republic and was elected its first President in October 1923 (re-elected 1927, 1931 and 1935). Pushed through reforms – abolition of Caliphate and disestablishment of Islam in 1924, ban on wearing of fez, and suppression of religious orders in 1925, adoption of Swiss Civil Code in 1926, introduction of Latin script in 1926, adoption of western-type surnames in 1934 (when Mustafa Kemal chose the name of Atatürk, i.e. 'Father of the Turks'). Gained province of Hatay (Alexandretta) from French-mandated Syria in 1937-8. Posthumously proclaimed 'Eternal Leader' in December 1939.

CELÂL BAYAR (1884–   ) Prime Minister, then third President of the Turkish Republic. His father was a country town mufti. At the age of twenty-three Celâl made history by becoming manager of the Bursa branch of a German Bank. At the same time he joined the Young Turks' party, becoming later head of its local organization in Izmir, a position which he used in 1919 to mount resistance against the invading Greeks. Elected Deputy in the National Assembly in Ankara. He played after the war a leading role in shaping financial and economic policy, first as Director General of the Government-sponsored commercial bank and then, between 1932 and 1937, as Minister of Economy. In 1937 he replaced Inönü as Prime Minister thus starting a feud which went on for over thirty years. A founder of the Democratic Party in 1945, he was elected President of the Republic in 1950, and ejected by the army in 1960. After the military coup he was condemned to death, reprieved and finally released into disapproving private retirement.

BAYEZID I Called Yıldırım, 'the Thunderbolt' (1354–1403) Ottoman Sultan. In 1389 he succeeded his father Murad I who had been mortally wounded at the Battle of Kosovo, at which the Serbs were defeated. Bayezid first tried to control the Balkans through local Christian princes, including the Byzantine Emperor of Constantinople. However, many of these princes turned to the West for help and a crusade against the Ottomans was organized by Hungary and Venice. In 1396 Bayezid defeated the crusaders at Nicopolis (Niğbolu) and ordered the blockade of Constantinople, while himself going east to add to his domains in Anatolia those of adjacent Turkish princes. This brought him into conflict with Tamerlane (Timur Leng) who defeated and captured Bayezid at the battle of Ankara in 1402.

BAYEZID II (c. 1447–1512) Ottoman Sultan. He succeeded his father Mehmed II the Conqueror, after defeating his brother Jem. Bayezid added Herzegovina and the mouth of the Danube to the Empire. He was the architect of Ottoman naval power in the Mediterranean; he defeated Venice, depriving it of most of its castles in the Balkans. In 1512 he was forced to abdicate in favour of his son Selim I the Grim, sworn enemy of the Shiites who were at that time threatening the integrity of the Ottoman possessions in Asia Minor.

OSMAN BÖLÜKBAŞI (1913–) Leader of Nation Party, a small nationalist right-wing group. A mathematician by training, he built up a considerable personal following by his attacks first on Menderes and the Democrats, then on Inönü. A thorn in the flesh of every government, even those in which his party took part, he is one of the most colourful parliamentarians and the most vigorous orators in Turkey.

ALI FUAD CEBESOY (1882–1968) Turkish commander and one of the leaders of Anatolian resistance. Was Commander of Central Anatolian Army Corps after the 1918 armistice. His H.Q. was in Ankara where he invited Mustafa Kemal (Atatürk) when the latter arrived in Anatolia to organize Turkish national resistance. Kemal made him Western Front Commander. Later after a disagreement on the role of partisans in military operations, Atatürk sent him to Moscow as Ambassador. A brief experiment in opposition led to his retirement from politics until after Atatürk's death when he became Minister and finally President of the Assembly.

CEMAL PASHA (Djemal Pasha) (1872–1922) Military politician and Young Turk leader. At the time of the 1908 coup he was railway inspector in Macedonia. After the coup he held several governorates, was an unsuccessful commander in the Balkan war; then after the consolidation of the Young Turkish dictatorship in 1913, he became Military Governor of Istanbul and later Navy Minister. Without relinquishing his office in the cabinet, he was from 1914 to 1917 military governor of Syria and Commander of the 4th Army in Damascus. He is remembered for having ordered the hanging of thirty-two prominent Arabs on charges of conspiring with the enemy. After the armistice of 1918, he fled first to Berlin and then to Soviet Russia. He was assassinated in Tiflis by two Armenians, bent on avenging the massacres of Armenians under the Young Turks.

SÜLEYMAN DEMIREL (1924–) Turkish Prime Minister 1965– . Born in a peasant household in the province of Isparta (SW Turkey), he was trained as a civil engineer at the Istanbul Technical University. After further training in the USA, he joined the Civil Service, becoming Director of State Water Board and surnamed 'King of Dams'. After the 1960 coup he worked briefly, but very successfully, as a private contractor, then entered politics, being almost immediately elected leader of the Justice Party. Deputy Prime Minister in the Ürgüplü caretaker government in February 1965, he became Prime Minister after his party's victory in the general elections held in October that year. The following year, Turkey's economic development reached the highest rate ever recorded.

BÜLENT ECEVIT (1925–) Secretary General of Republican Peoples' Party since 1966, and champion of its left-of-centre policy. An intellectual in politics, he was Minister of Labour between 1961 and 1965 when strikes and collective bargaining were legalized.

ENVER PASHA (1881–1922) Young Turk military politician. At the Young Turk coup of 1908, Enver, who was then a major, was acclaimed as a hero of liberty, as he had, a month earlier, fled to the hills, when his conspiratorial activities had come to the notice of the authorities. After the revolution he spent two years as military attaché in Berlin before going to Libya to fight the Italians. In January 1913, in the middle of the Balkan war, he organized a second Young Turk coup in Istanbul, which put an end to parliamentary rule and also to Ottoman rule over the remaining parts of Macedonia. However, in July of the same year, Enver once again emerged as a hero, when he profited from the defeat of the Bulgarians in the Second Balkan war, in order to re-occupy Edirne for the Turks. In 1914 he was promoted General and appointed Minister of War and at the outbreak of World War I, he became Deputy (i.e. Acting) C-in-C. He was largely responsible for bringing the Ottoman Empire into the war, on the side of Germany, for introducing a large number of German officers into the Ottoman forces, for killing off the Ottoman 3rd Army in the disastrous Sarikamiş operation on the Russian front, and for an attempt to form a Great Turan, largely at the expense of the Russian Empire. After the armistice he fled to Berlin, then to Soviet Russia. After futile attempts to gain control of the Anatolian resistance movement from Mustafa Kemal Atatürk, who would not have him in the country, Enver went to Uzbekistan, where breaking with the Bolsheviks, he tried to take command of Central Asian Muslim nationalists. He was killed in an engagement with Soviet Russian troops not far from the Afghan border. To Atatürk, Enver was the prototype of the irresponsible adventurers who had brought the Ottoman Empire to its knees.

TURHAN FEYZIOĞLU (1922–) Leader of Reliance Party. He broke with the Republican Peoples' Party in 1967, condemning its left-of-centre policy as an attempt to dragoon the people. He had risen to prominence in the fifties as an outspoken critic of Menderes when he was forced to relinquish his chair at the School of Political Science in Ankara.

ZIYA GÖKALP (c. 1875–1924) Chief ideologist of Turkish nationalism. Born in Diyarbakir he joined the Young Turk conspirators, was briefly imprisoned, and after 1908 emerged as the chief publicist and mentor of the Young Turkish Party. After the war he switched his support to Mustafa Kemal Atatürk. Gökalp's views changed during his life, as his purpose was to provide a philosophical justification for the defence of what was left to be defended. Thus after toying with Ottomanism, Pan-Islamism and Pan-Turanianism he settled for Turkish nationalism, more or less within the limits of Atatürk's republic.

CEMAL GÜRSEL (1890–1966) Fourth President of the Turkish Republic. A career officer, he was Commander of Land Forces in the last days of Menderes. He made known his opposition to Menderes and withdrew to his private house in Izmir, to re-emerge shortly afterwards as head of the National Unity Committee, the junta which took over on 27 May 1960. The plotters chose him as the most senior officer sympathetic to them, although he had taken no part in the preparation of the coup. Inside the junta Gürsel threw his weight on the side of those who wanted a return to parliamentary rule, and after the free elections of October 1961, he was rewarded by being elected President of the Republic. Under his guidance power was gradually and smoothly transferred from the enemies to the successors of Menderes. After suffering a stroke in March 1966 he was declared permanently unfit to perform his duties. He died in September of the same year.

ISMET İNÖNÜ (1884–   ) Second President of the Turkish Republic and original licensing authority of Turkish parliamentary democracy. Born in Izmir in W Turkey, he had a military education and first worked with Mustafa Kemal (Atatürk) on the Russian front in 1916 when he became Kemal's Chief of Staff. It was more or less this function which he performed for the next thirty years. He joined Kemal in Ankara in 1920 to become first Chief of Staff and then Commander of the Western Front, in which capacity he twice defeated the Greeks near the village of İnönü, whence his surname. After the war he became Foreign Minister and as such, Chief Turkish delegate at the Lausanne Peace Conference. With the proclamation of the Republic he was appointed Prime Minister, a post which he kept, except for a brief interval in 1925, until 1937 when he was replaced by Celâl Bayar (q.v.). He became President of the Republic after Atatürk's death in 1938, and after keeping Turkey out of World War II and presiding over the change-over to political democracy withdrew into opposition in 1950. He made a vigorous leader of the opposition, manœuvred Menderes and his Democrats into an impasse, and then led the military junta out of one, when he became Prime Minister in 1961. Having helped to lay the foundations of the Second Republic, as he had of the First, he was once again forced into opposition in 1965.

KÂZIM KARABEKIR (1882–1948) Commander of Ottoman forces in Erzurum at the beginning of Mustafa Kemal's Anatolian campaign. Kemal confirmed him in his position by designating him Commander of the Eastern Front, in which capacity he defeated the Armenian Nationalist Republic. He remained virtually master of Eastern Anatolia until 1923. After the war he went into opposition to Kemal, was tried on a charge of complicity in an attempt on Kemal's life, was acquitted and ended his life in the honorific position of President of the National Assembly.

MAHMUD II (1784–1839) The first modern Ottoman Sultan. He destroyed the Janissaries, organized a modern army, introduced a new type of headgear (always the mark of a reformer), opened new schools, sent students to Europe and started a newspaper. He also lost Greece (up to Thessaly), Serbia and (all but in name) Egypt.

MAHMUT MAKAL (1925–) Turkish schoolteacher who attained literary and political fame with the publication of his account of rural life *Bizim Köy* (*Our Village*). He is the author of several books on rural themes and is active in progressive left-wing causes.

MEHMED II the Conqueror (1432–1481) Ottoman Sultan. After conquering Constantinople in 1453 and transferring his capital there, he added Trabzon (Trebizond), the Morea (Peleponnese) and other large tracts of the Balkans and of Asia Minor to his possessions. He was consciously an imperial monarch, an organizer of the Ottoman Empire and a patron of religious learning and the arts.

ADNAN MENDERES (1899–1961) Turkish Prime Minister 1950–60. A landowner near Aydın, W Turkey, he was educated at the new Ankara Faculty of Law and entered politics at an early age as a Deputy of the ruling Republican People's Party. He resigned in 1945, objecting to a measure of land reform, and became one of the founders of the Democratic Party, whose victory earned him the post of Prime Minister. He led Turkey into the Western Alliance, the Korean War, and a spurt of inflationary, but electorally popular development, which, as he was fond of saying himself was 'unequalled' in Turkish history. He quickly outran the country's resources and the esteem of the élite, which then inspired the armed forces to the coup of 27 May 1960. His trial failed to destroy his popular reputation and his execution by the military made of him a martyr of democracy in the eyes of millions of Turks, while making way for less frenetic successors.

MURAD I (c. 1326–89) Ottoman Sultan. He conquered Edirne (Adrianople) where he transferred his capital and laid the foundations of Ottoman rule in the Balkans. He died on the battlefield of Kosovo, where he had dealt a mortal blow to the Serbian kingdom.

MURAD II (1403–50) Ottoman Sultan. He extended Ottoman rule in the Balkans and in Asia Minor and, by defeating Hunyadi's crusaders at the battle of Varna in 1444, he consolidated previous gains and sealed the fate of Constantinople.

NAMIK KEMAL (1840–88) Turkish 'poet of Liberty', national poet, journalist and dramatist. A leading Young Ottoman, he spent three years in exile in Europe. His best-known literary work is the patriotic play *Vatan Yahut Silistre* (*The Fatherland or Silistria*). The Young Turks considered him their chief inspiration.

NAZIM HIKMET (1902–63) Turkish communist poet. He came from a distinguished Ottoman family of high functionaries, was educated at the lycée of Galatasaray and the Naval Academy in Istanbul, quickly became known as a writer of 'syllabic' (as against 'quantitative') verse and was one of a small group of avant-garde poets who joined Mustafa Kemal in Anatolia. There he soon came into conflict with a careful local nationalism, and went on to Moscow in pursuit of his generous vision of Utopia. After completing his education at the Eastern Workers' University he returned to Istanbul to be lionized by progressive salons, attacked by right-wing nationalists and finally imprisoned for fourteen years for allegedly spreading sedition among the armed forces. Amnestied in 1950, he fled to Eastern Europe never to return. Prolific, zestful, romantic, he was cast in the mould of a nineteenth-century literary revolutionary. Turkish literature has come to be grateful for his vigour, his daring innovations with style and prosody and above all for his craftsmanlike use of spoken Turkish, which this rebel poet treated with greater respect and patience than did his conformist contemporaries.

ORHAN KEMAL (1914–   ) Prolific Turkish writer of short and long-short stories. He spent his childhood in the Lebanon where his father had fled as a right-wing conservative opponent of Atatürk. Orhan Kemal himself developed in the opposite direction to become the doyen of left-wing writers. A romantic left-wing humanist, he shares with his peers and imitators a compassion for the fate of 'little men', which is ultimately derived from Chekhov.

ORKHAN (Orhan) (1281–1362) Ottoman Sultan. He reduced the NW corner of Asia Minor, including Izmit (Nicomedeia) and Iznik (Nicaea). His son Süleyman Pasha crossed the Dardanelles and captured Gallipoli.

OSMAN I (1258–1326) Founder of Ottoman dynasty. In 1281 he inherited from his father Ertruğrul a small ghazi principality on the banks of the Sakarya river between Ankara and Bursa, which he extended westwards at the expense of the Byzantines. Bursa fell to his son Orkhan in 1326. Osman died in the same year.

SAIT FAIK (1907–54) Turkey's best-known writer of short stories which almost invariably describe life in Istanbul in the late 'thirties and 'forties and often have for their heroes Greek fishermen and tradesmen. A romantic and compassionate craftsman working on a small scale, Sait Faik is implicitly a critic of the quality of life in an impoverished metropolis.

SELIM I the Grim (c. 1467–1520) Ottoman Sultan. In 1512 he forced his father Bayezid to abdicate in his favour. At the battle of Çaldıran (1514) he defeated the Shiite menace in Asia Minor, adding to the Empire the SE provinces of the present Turkish Republic. He then destroyed the Mamluk power in Egypt and Syria which were also incorporated in the Ottoman Empire.

SELIM II (c. 1524–74) Known as the Drunkard. Ottoman Sultan whose reign saw the Ottoman conquest of the Yemen and Cyprus (1571), but also the defeat of the Ottoman fleet at Lepanto (1571).

SELIM III (1761–1809) Ottoman Sultan. His attempt to form a Western-style new army (Nizam-ı cedid) cost him his throne and his life, but led nevertheless to the reforms of his westernizing successors.

SÜLEYMAN I the Magnificent or the Lawgiver (1495–1566) Ottoman Sultan
184

whose reign witnessed the apogee of the Empire. He resumed the advance westwards, capturing Rhodes (1522) and inflicting a crushing defeat on the Hungarians (1526). In 1534 he captured Baghdad which, except for a brief period (1623–38) was to remain in Ottoman hands until 1917. But he failed to take Vienna in 1529 or Malta in 1565.

CEVDET SUNAY (1900–   ) Fifth President of the Turkish Republic. Born in Trabzon. He is a career officer who fought on the Palestine Front in World War I and subsequently rose in the military hierarchy, becoming Chief of General Staff in 1960. After the 1960 coup he sided with the constitutionalists against the radicals and helped suppress the two attempted putsches of Col. Aydemir. His election to the Presidency in March 1966 was supported by all the main political parties.

TALAT PASHA (Talaat Pasha) (1872–1921) Young Turkish leader and Ottoman Prime Minister in the last stages of World War I. He fled after the armistice and was assassinated by an Armenian nationalist.

ALPASLAN TÜRKEŞ (1917–) Leader of the right-wing radical Republican Peasants and Nation Party, is a military politician who has lived dangerously. Born in Cyprus and trained in the army, he was arrested at the end of World War II for his alleged involvement in the pro-German Panturanian racialist movement. He emerged in May 1960 as one of the most active plotters of the coup, and became its chief spokesman. His advocacy of nationalist discipline (through his One Culture movement) alarmed his more moderate colleagues, and with thirteen other radical officers, he was expelled from the junta and exiled. On his return he captured control of the small RPNP and was elected to Parliament from the pool of 'wasted votes'.

YAŞAR KEMAL (1922–) Left-wing romantic Turkish writer of novels on rural themes. He comes from a Kurdish-Turkoman family of some standing which had been exiled to a village near Adana. He received very little formal education and after a hard childhood rose to literary fame by way of journalism. He substituted epic tales of revolt for sad little vignettes as a vehicle for social protest and was rewarded by large sales both in Turkey and abroad, where he is probably the best-known living Turkish writer.

Acknowledgements

The photographs used in this book are by Sonia Halliday, except the following: Robert Blomfield, 18, 20; British Museum: Melchior Lorch, *Costumes, etc. (1570–83)* 2; British Petroleum Company Ltd., 33; Camera Press, 9, 13, (Rene Noorbergen) 12, 14, (Lisa Larsen) 15, (Philippe Andrieu) 24, (Gérard Décaux) 30; Giraudon, 3, 4; Keystone Press, 11; Radio Times Hulton Picture Library, 6; Turkish Embassy, 10, 19, 29, 31, 32, 34; Photo Yan, 16.

Index

Numbers in italic refer to illustrations

189

Konya, 14, 15, 17, 21, 45, 119, 150, 151, 159
Korean War, 74, 75, 77
Kurds, 12, 29, 32, 39, 53, 54, 63, 99, 100, 103–105, 138, 140, 143, 150
Kütahya, 46

LANGUAGE reform, 60, 61
Lausanne, Treaty of, 52, 63, 64
Lazes, 39, 141
Literature, 121–124
Little Ararat, 138
Lydians, 12

MACEDONIA, 30, 41
Maeander river, 137
Mahmud II (see Who's Who, p. 182), 27
Makal, Mahmut (see Who's Who, p. 182), 123
Malatya, 100
Malazgirt, 14, 15, 16
Malta, 22
Mamluks, 22
Manisa, 18
Mardin, 100, 143
Marmaris, 142
Marshall Plan, 74
Matveyev, 137
Medical services, 124, 125
Mehmed II (see Who's Who, p. 182), 21
Mejid, Abdul, see Abdul Mejid I
Menderes, Adnan (see Who's Who, p. 182), 71, 74–79, 93–98, 127, 128, 145, 157, 163, 11
Menteshe, 18
Meriç river, 146
Mersin, 142, 143, 144, 159, 162
Mevlevi, 17, 39, 151, 6
Milâs, 137
Miletus, 137, 145
Molotov, 69
Mongols, 13, 16, 17, 20
Montreux, Convention of, 63, 69
Mosque of Süleyman the Magnificent, 1
Murad I (see Who's Who, p. 183), 20
Murad II (see Who's Who, p. 183), 21

Muş, 42, 139
Mussolini, 63

NAKSHIBENDIS, 39, 53, 54
Namık Kemal (see Who's Who, p. 183), 122
National Covenant, 40, 44
NATO, 75, 166, 167
Nazım Hikmet (see Who's Who, p. 183), 123
Nevşehir, 150
Nicaea, 14, 18
Nicomedeia, see Izmit
Nicopolis, see Niğbolu
Niğbolu, 20

OEEC, 75, 167
Oğuz Turks, 13, 14
Orbay, Rauf, 53
Orhan Kemal (see Who's Who, p. 184), 59, 123
Orkhan (see Who's Who, p. 184), 18
Ortahisar rock dwellings, 27
Osman, 18
Osman I (see Who's Who, p. 184), 131
Otranto, 21

PAKISTAN, 75
Palaologi, 19
Pamphylia, 136, 142
Peloponnese, 21
Peoples' Party, see Republican Peoples' Party
Pergamum, 145
Persia(ns), 11–13, 16, 19, 22, 63, 75, 103, 121, 138, 139
Peter the Great, 27
Phrygians, 12
Polatkan, Hasan, 77
Pontus, 22
Population, 65, 70, 72, 152
Populism, 56
Porsuk river, 140
Progressive Party, 53, 57
Proussa, see Bursa

RAMANDAĞ, 159